Moving Out of the Dark

by

Andy Pacino

Version 1

Contents

1st Edition 2021

Published by No Ordinary Family

ISBN: 978-1-7399096-0-4

Dedication

One of the worst phrases I've ever heard is "successful suicide." To think that this awful term has made it into our vocabulary is shocking. To think that a completed suicide could ever be described as successful is just madness in my eyes. Death in itself is usually tragic, but for someone ending their own life due to mental breakdown is more than tragic; it's heartbreaking, it's decimating and it's also life-changing for the families who survive the so-called successful suicide.

This book is dedicated to those who struggle with their day-to-day existence. Survival is the most natural of our instincts, and when we let go of that, we lose also our perspective of life and its value. When those who are down think of their own lives, they think of them as not being worthy of continuing. That is almost certainly never the case.

The devastation that suicide leaves is immeasurable, yet the levels of such rival cancer and heart disease in certain demographics, certainly among ex-armed forces, middle aged men, and alienated parents who have had their children all but illegally snatched from them by partners who would rather see a child have less love than see their ex build a loving relationship with their child, which, having been though it myself, I find both evil and staggering.

I have given as much background information to each of the accounts as possible in order to investigate as fully as possible what might bring on suicidal feelings, and I hope it also helps the reader get a handle on the contributors and their personalities, which some people might recognise in themselves. If there is one thing I have learnt through interviewing, transcribing and editing this book, it is that no matter how low you might feel, no matter how much you might think the world would be better off without you, you're wrong. For those of you who think there is no one to speak to, you are wrong again. There is always someone who cares enough to listen, just as there is always someone who will make you feel worse about yourself if you allow them to.

To those of you in turmoil, I ask you to seek out someone who you know; someone who you are friends with, and who you might speak to sporadically, or a member of your family. Let them know how you feel. None of those with whom I chatted outside of this book, as well as those who I interviewed during the process of producing this book, don't wish that their loved one who killed themselves had spoken to them before they took their own life.

Below is a website that contains a list of helplines you can call from wherever in the world you live.

http://www.suicide.org/international-suicide-hotlines.html

Introduction And Disclaimer

The sources this book was drawn from are all genuine. The stories contained within are also all genuine. Contributors have given their accounts of how suicide or attempted suicide has affected them and their families, and while Neil James, John Fioriantes and Lakshmi Khan's accounts have been made anonymous with geographical locations and names changed, Mandy Crossland, Mark Dale and Luke Scott's accounts have not. All three of the latter contributors now work or volunteer for mental health help groups or organisations, and each has contributed in the hope of saving even one life, or one family from the grief caused by the effects of suicide.

These accounts are given in response to a request I made for contributors, and are not meant to be an exhaustive list of all situations where people may be considering suicide. Rather, it is about people going through severe depression and coming out the other side still relatively intact, regardless of the circumstances that put them there in the first place.

The author accepts no responsibility for accuracy or details in the accounts, and this book has been published on the proviso that all contributors have given honest and true accounts of their experience with how suicide has affected them and/or their families.

Acknowledgements

My gratitude goes out to the contributors to this book. The accounts within moved me and helped me on both a personal and professional level, and I thank each and very one of you for sharing your experience and journey with the readers and me. If it helps only one person, it will have been worth it.

I would also like to offer thanks to Dr Kirin Hilliar for her invaluable input and advice.

One: John Fioriantes, 46, Bedfordshire

Let me say this before we start: anyone whose life becomes affected by suicide will lead a shitty existence that they will never truly get over.

I was the younger of two brothers to a single parent who had led a stylish life as a dancer in a quite famous dance troupe on a cruise liner. She was one of those archetypical dancers; long legs, long, dark curly hair, piercing blue eyes, slim and very good-looking. When she was around 28 she hooked up with one of the ship's crew members who was by all accounts a dashing, olive-skinned guy who had an eye for the ladies, with my mum being one of them. They weren't together for that long – two, maybe three years at the most. Mum, bless her, had her dancing life cut short when she got pregnant with my elder brother, Paul, bringing an end to an otherwise exciting life of travelling from country to country entertaining cruise liner guests. My dad, if I can call him that, didn't stick around once I appeared on the scene.

When I was born Paul was just about at the learning-to-walk stage, and there were no signs of his ensuing life of turmoil dealing with what doctors would later diagnose as paranoid schizophrenia. That would surface around the age of five or six, and it meant that my childhood would be anything other than normal. As I knew no other life than my own and in my house with my grandparents, mum and Paul, what I thought was normal didn't bear any resemblance to other people's normal lives. For me, normal life was getting home from school and finding my brother waiting for me behind a door and attacking me the moment I walked into the house. The fights we had weren't usual sibling scrap either: he would properly try to hurt me. Once he held my arm between two stairs and knelt on it with a lot of force trying to break it. That wasn't anything out of the ordinary though; while gardening on another occasion, he threw a garden fork at my face. It narrowly missed my eye but it did catch my forehead and I had to have seven stiches. I still carry the scar with me today. That meant I grew up thinking people were hostile and that I had to learn to fight very quickly or I would suffer the consequences, and I fought at school the moment I saw trouble, or thought that it might be brewing. I had the mentality of "hit first", to make sure I walked away unhurt. Unfortunately, it also meant I didn't have that many friends, and I didn't know how to form proper relationships.

When I was around six my mum, still a pretty attractive woman, got married again and my new stepdad, Keith, was a great guy who treated Paul and me like we were his own. They didn't have any other kids together and I never felt there was anything even remotely near resentment from him, and we did the family days out and holidays. The only difficulty we had was dealing with Paul's "episodes". He got into more than his fare share of trouble at school and it wasn't long before he was deemed a little too hot to handle, and he got expelled from one school after another until none of them would have him.

At home he was an absolute fucking nightmare to live with. I dreaded going back there after school because Mom and Keith were both out at work, and Paul would inevitably be lying in wait for me after setting up yet another elaborate ambush. For so much of the time I spent with him, I never knew which Paul I was going to meet when I got home. Bedtimes were also something of a chore as he slept in the bottom bunk and insisted on kicking the shit out of my bed from below, often lifting the bedstead out of its slots that kept one on top of the other, and more than once it collapsed on him. On the one hand I hated him, but he was my brother, and despite all of his psychological and personal problems, I loved him too.

By the time I got to high school I understood he was also a manic depressive, which is now known as bipolar disorder, and although I didn't fully realise what the term meant, it manifested itself in a number of his suicide attempts followed by hospital stays and a month or two's stays in mental health wards. More than anything else that affected me at school was Paul's will to kill himself, as word got out it wasn't long before I was known as Nutty Paul's brother rather than plain old John Fiориantes.

I was the one whose brother was always trying to "off" himself, and kids – and even those few I had managed to strike up some form of a friendship with – could be quite cruel and I got a tremendous amount of shit for it, though what I could do about it wasn't much, other than fight. Fortunately for me, due to my constant battles with him and having to protect myself from Paul's often flying knuckles and feet, I got handier with my fists and it didn't take long before the majority of the other kids at school got wise and decided to give me the widest berth they could find and leave me well alone.

Around the time I was in Year 11 and getting ready

for my GCSEs, I was called into the headmaster, Mr. Morton's, office, and he told me that I had to go home as quickly as I could. I asked him what was wrong and why I had to go but he wouldn't say anything other than he didn't know but it was urgent. When I got home mum's car was outside, which was unusual as she should have been at work, and there was a police car there too. I racked my brain wondering what it was I must have done wrong, and once I got inside I saw Mum sat on a chair crying into a handkerchief, and a policewoman rubbing her back and comforting her.

Keith, Nan and Granddad were also there and so I knew it wasn't anything to do with something I might have done. I knew it must be Paul, even though he wasn't there. I was really confused. Had he been arrested? Was he in hospital? My nan came towards me and opened her arms to give me a hug, and I asked what was wrong, what had happened? She told me softly that there had been a problem with Paul and that he had thrown himself off a high rise building in the city centre, and that he was dead.

I was flabbergasted. I didn't know how to react. He had tried a couple of times to off himself previously though they were pills and drink; the first attempt being when he tried strangling himself, though none of them were successful. After the time he tried to hang himself he was put into an institution for a while until they said he was fit enough to leave, though even then I saw no evidence of him having changed in the slightest other than being a little more stupefied than usual, though I guessed that was from the medication he'd been prescribed. For his second attempt he swallowed the lot of his own meds as well as a bottle each of Mum's Mogadon and Valium with half a bottle of something called Clan Dew, which I think was a kind of whisky, and he was whisked off to the Larch Ward at Waterloo Manor in Leeds again. I guess it was always going to be just a matter of time before he did it properly, if I can use that term.

The morning he killed himself proper had been no different to any other. He was as normal as he had ever been, and as far as I knew he'd been taking his meds and was as levelled out as he could be, and he seemed fine. We found out some weeks later from a couple of mutual friends that the night before he killed himself that he'd had a few beers on his own at The Viaduct, which was a gay bar on Briggate, although he wasn't gay, and then he went on to a club and came home around 4am. I heard him get into bed while I pretended to be asleep. The next day I got ready for school and off I went and the rest is now part of the family history.

Our family life was wrecked pretty much instantly. The guilt we all felt collectively for not being able to help was horrible. It was stifling and none of us got over it, and it still bothers me to this day, twenty odd years later. Mum went into depression, she and Keith argued, and they almost split up a couple of times. It was only down to his enormous strength of character and personal resilience that they stayed together. He was a fucking rock at the time and I cannot ever thank him enough for the way he supported my mum and me.

It took quite a few years longer for the gravity of it to sink in with me, and I felt a huge amount of guilt as I was the one he fought with more than anyone else, and I wondered if it was because I hadn't handled him better that he killed himself. I now know that's not the case, of course, but I tortured myself with it constantly when I was younger. I struggled, and first I turned to dope and some while later I took my first hit of smack via a matchbox and tin foil, and from that moment on I was a mess for the larger part of my life.

I went to university and studied philosophy, partly

because I wanted to try and get some kind of understanding and partly because I heard that it was mainly females who took philosophy courses. The women took a back seat though, as my only relationship at the time was with heroin. All through my time there I stuck needles in my arm trying to blot out Paul's death.

It wasn't long before I became depressed too, and there were countless occasions when I was at some seriously low points that I thought if I just poured a little more than usual into myself that I too would die, though it would seem more like an overdoes than a suicide and that it would be easier for my family to handle if it were an accidental OD being the case of my death.

Each time I thought that this would be the last time, and each time I woke again, more often than not in a mess, quite often in a pool of puke from the previous night's intake of booze and smack. I changed degrees from philosophy to psychology to try to get a further insight into both Paul's mental state, his death, and my own depression, and it was while I was training to be a counsellor that I managed to find some clarity to my situation and come to terms with the fact that I wasn't to blame and that my own depression was linked not only to Paul's death, but also from a feeling of not knowing who I was due to my dad's disappearance when I was a kid. I never thought that had anything to do with my mental state, because I had such a loving upbringing from my mum and Keith, and never realised that my need for an identity would surface like in the way it did.

That wasn't the end of my trouble though. After I left university I took another degree and got into electronics and worked on some of the biggest engineering projects in the UK, and I was trusted with some very, very expensive equipment that had I messed up, could have caused lots of death and untold disaster. The main problem was that I was still a junkie. In a normal life, a junkie can function perfectly well as long as they have the means to buy their gear, and life could almost be considered normal. However, there was an occasion I bought a wrap of heroin that was laced with strychnine.

It sounds ridiculous, doesn't it, but that's what happened. I'm not going to go into details, there's no point, but the upshot was that I threw a wobbler of titanic proportions and almost killed myself and a load of colleagues in the process. I got fired pretty quickly, spent every penny I'd managed to save even quicker on a binge of smack, weed, ecstasy and alcohol, and once again thought of giving myself a giant hit to call it a day.

The levels on mental health issues and a whole host of other problems multiply ten-fold when you're a smackhead. And when you're already dealing with monsters in your head it is much worse. I was sick of my monsters and so I decided I wasn't going to live with them any longer. It was a Friday night and I'd been drinking throughout the day, so I was sailing three sheets to the wind by the time I went to a club. I was hammered.

Throughout the evening I dropped around nine ecstasy pills (Es) and danced in a stupor for much of that night and into the early morning of the Saturday. After kicking out time at around 9 am, I called my dealer and bought the last batch of heroin that he had; five wraps, which was around half a gram, though his gear was usually better than most other dealers' stuff. That meant it should do the trick and then some.

I got back to my flat, and made myself one last cup of tea: it was Brook Bond PG Tips (monkey tea for a monkey fool, I guess). I used two tea bags as I thought that if I'm going to off myself, I might as well have one last strong cup of tea before I go. I cooked up, again, I won't go through the process, and sucked the liquid into a needle before injecting it into a vein in my foot. The veins in my arms had scabbed up and I'd had difficulty finding a decent entry point the day before. I drifted off in peace, and wondered what death would be like.

When morning struck I peeled open my eyes due to the gunk that had amassed around them, and yet again I was soaked in thin, alcohol and smack-induced puke. Adding insult to the already unbearable injury, I had also well and truly shit myself. Talk about degrading. I decided to leave my flat for good, and see if I could starve myself to death instead. I have no idea why that thought entered my head: I still don't understand it to this day.

I made a beeline to the Embankment along the River Thames, wandered around for the rest of the day feeling very sorry for myself, and once evening struck I wrapped myself in as much cardboard as I could find. Thinking back to then, I wonder why I did that because the sole idea in my head was to die. I'd heard that freezing to death was one of the more pleasant ways to end it all, as when hypothermia sets in you lose a grasp of reality and slowly drift off into a peaceful, never ending sleep.

However, I didn't manage to make it that far. Two weeks later I was still clinging to life, although to look at me you wouldn't think so. In fact, it was only when I looked at this tramp who was staring at me from inside a shop that I realised the tramp was me, and I was scoffing at my own reflection. It shocked me into thinking I could still have a chance at life and that I shouldn't feel the way I did about myself. I was a double Bachelor degree holder, I wasn't stupid, and I might even be able to turn myself back into a human again. Again?

I still have no idea how I managed to get myself together, but I did, and I got myself a Government-sponsored (it kept me off their unemployment figures) English teaching certificate, and from there I went to South America teaching English to office workers who wanted to sell goods in the West and needed language skills to do so. While I was in Columbia, not the best place in the world for me to be in, I hooked up with a woman who was possibly almost as fucked up as I was, but incredibly we both got clean(ish) together. She has been there for me while I've been in some of my darkest places and even now, another ten years after I left Columbia, I still go from day to day. I still hit the smack now and again, actually we both do, and sometimes I wonder if my mental state will ever revert to the way I felt way back, and the honest answer is I don't know.

I'm not sure there were warning signs for someone in my heroin-addicted condition, but prior to that there were plenty of other pointers; I didn't trust people, I didn't make friends easily, I drank too much, I got into too many fights for no reason, my moods were up and down all the time, and I think if I'd had just one person whom I could turn and talk to, life may have been different for me. That probably sounds harsh on my mum and Keith, but in all honesty I didn't feel I could heap even more pressure on them than I had. They'd already gone through so much with my brother, but thinking about it, I guess I could and should have done. Another dead son may have been too much for them to bear.

My one piece of advice for anyone thinking of taking their own life is speak to someone. Open up to your best friend or your brother or sister and if they don't want to listen to you, find someone else who will. The suicide rate among junkies is ridiculous, and with men who aren't junkies it is increasing at a crazy rate. From what I can see, not enough is being done about it, although advances in help and welfare are being made slowly. There are self-help groups, anonymous helplines like the Samaritans and people out there who don't know you, but they could be the ones to save your life and help you make your existence a little more normal or at least liveable.

Unfortunately, your GP will usually only be a stop gap, and from personal experience I can tell you there's a long waiting list to see a counsellor on the NHS unless you make an attempt on your life. But that could be, and often is, too late for some.

John Fioriantes, 46, Bedfordshire

Two: Mandy Crossland, 43, Suffolk

Chris and I met when I was on the main gate of a military installation in Basra, Iraq, in 2004. I'd been in the Royal Air Force (RAF) as a Ministry of Defence (MoD) police officer for a couple of years and the first moment I saw him I liked him. He was a happy man, his smile was as wide as his face and he lit up the area whenever he spoke. He was cheeky, funny, witty, and his sense of humour was very much in tune with my own. To say he had the gift of the gab would be an understatement, and he could charm the minerals from a rock. He was a typical man's man, and while he wasn't politically correct, neither was he vicious or rude. He had no qualms about being who he was and his friends and colleagues admired him for it.

You always knew where you stood with him. Some of his friends would refer to him as a social hand grenade, because if there was a posh do on, he could end up offending someone or other with his bluntness. He never meant to cause offence, but his naive honesty raised eyebrows on more than occasion. We had a bit of a whirlwind romance and then we got married. During the first couple of years we had an amazing amount of fun, and I loved being with him. Just under two years later our son, Jamie, arrived and he was an absolute bundle of joy. I loved having him, though it did mean I had little other choice than to give up my career in the RAF.

As Chris and I were both in the armed forces, the pair of us understood that there would be a lot of time spent apart. At one point in time you could be in the army for 30 years and, other than a tour or two of Northern Ireland tackling the IRA, never see armed conflict, however, after the first Gulf War it seems as though the British have been fighting conflicts on many fronts with different enemies, and Chris saw way more than his fair share of ugliness.

I understood quite early on that he was living with psychological problems, as he often had nightmares and would start screaming in the middle of the night, or I would have to wake him up due to his arms and legs flailing and him shouting while he was having a nightmare. That brought him out from the pain of his subconscious that took him back to his grisly past as he slept. Although it was a little scary, there was never too much trouble with that, as he would talk matters through in the morning and tell me what was on his mind.

He understood that as an ex-forces lass, I had some

kind of insight into what he may have been through, even if I didn't know the full extent of where he'd been both mentally and physically. We had full trust in each other and although he had dealt with things on his own up until we got married, there was no need to bottle it up with me, which made me feel good. He didn't have the best start in life either: he was abandoned when he was only four years old. His mum dropped him off at his dad's house with a suitcase and after ringing the doorbell she told his dad that he had to take him on, as she was never going to find a husband while she had a kid with her, and while he didn't like to admit it, I think it affected him somewhat.

There were many occasions he spoke to me about his time in different fields of conflict, and how he'd seen his friends die in front of him during his time in Northern Ireland from around '94 to '97. Then there were the nightmares he had about his stints in Bosnia, Croatia, Serbia and then Kosovo a short time later. While on the outside he was a normal man, inside he must have been suffering, though he was quite obviously very good at locking it away in the recess of his mind. While he smiled and laughed, I still wonder how much he was crumbing inside. On occasion he would recall the times he'd seen the aftermath of execution sites where kids had been shot in the back or front of the head and laid out with their families and neighbours, who had been butchered wholesale. He had witnessed the death pits and mass graves, and spoken with people, men too, who had been the victims of gang rape.

The conflict in the Balkans went on for almost a decade, yet they are pretty much the forgotten wars in the West; let's not forget they went on from 1992 until almost the turn of the century, and that was a very grim reality for the men who had been there and tried to clean up the garbage left from either side hacking the other to pieces. Even bearing that in mind, he was always talkative and willing to share his thoughts and experiences and let me know how they made him feel. He trusted me with his past. We would explore his nightmares to see if there was a way we could move him away from them, it was as though talking about them brought them out into the open so they weren't locked away in his head any more.

When Chris got posted to Germany I moved over with him so that we could stay together. That time was pretty much OK for us; I could be a full-time mum and Chris would continue being a career Army man. He had been a soldier for quite a few years when we first met. As I mentioned, he'd served in Northern Ireland, Bosnia, Kosovo, as well as Sierra Leone, and while we were married he did a couple of stints in Iraq and then Afghanistan. Just before he went to Kenya in 2006 he tried to make out that he was disappointed with life in the forces, and that he was annoyed that we were going to be apart for so long, but I could see that for some reason there was another type of anger inside him. Even accounting for his dreams, his sleeping pattern had gone haywire and, perhaps in hindsight I should have seen that he wasn't so happy, and maybe that was the turning point in our relationship. Having said that, when he came home from Kenya he was fine again, and it was like he was back to the normal Chris. He was back to being exactly the man I fell in love with again. Maybe the sunshine had done him some good.

He went on his first tour of Afghanistan in 2008, and he left only six days after Jamie was born. He spent six months there and when he got back he threw himself into being a dad. He was great with Jamie and things between us were pretty good too. It was almost like a new start, because although we'd been married for quite a while, we had lived apart for most of it. He had spent most of his time on a base around two hours' drive away, and that meant he could afford to show me the side of his personality that he wanted to without having to put in too much effort.

His final tour was in Afghanistan at the tail end of 2011 and the beginning of 2012. At the time we were living in married quarters (MQs) in Munster, and once it was over he flew back into northern Germany, and then got a bus down to where we lived. I went to meet him and I took Jamie along as he was at the age when he was excited to see his dad. When the bus arrived both Jamie and I were looking forward to seeing him again, but as he stepped off the transport I instinctively knew something about him was different. He smiled his usual wide, beaming smile, but something I couldn't quite put my finger on was amiss: the grin wrinkles didn't quite reach his eyes. I could tell he wasn't a happy man. He was not happy at all.

With Chris, his eyes really were the doorway to his soul, and at this point the door was firmly fastened shut. His face looked dead, and he seemed bereft of emotion or happiness. I thought it would improve with time but it really didn't, and that frightened me. I could tell it wasn't the Chris I knew and loved. There was some part of him that was missing. I looked around me and watched how the other guys interacted with their wives and kids and they were different. With everyone else it was plainly obvious there was warmth and love; genuine happiness, but when I looked at Chris that wasn't evident at all. I wish I could explain it better.

He spoke, he laughed, he mingled, but it was like there was only the shell of himself, and inside he was empty. That night he got as drunk as a skunk, which of course I put down to the first night back from tour, and that is a common occurrence in the forces after being away so long. It's almost a celebration of life continuing. However it soon became clear he had gone from being a doting and loving dad and husband to an abusive and angry man. Being the closest person to him, he took his anger out on me, and for quite a while I thought I could work with him and bring him back to the person he was when we waved him off to his tour in 2012, but everything I tried was in vain. He drank to escape his demons and both the demons and his drinking got worse. When he drank he gambled, and as he was forever drunk, he was also forever posting money into fruit machines in the local pubs.

The difference between the first and second tour was

that things got a lot far more hairy during the second stint. His vehicle came very close to being hit by an IED, and I think that affected him. As much as I had promised myself I wouldn't watch the news reports I still did. I am certain that during that second tour something happened but he steadfastly refused to talk to me about it. While he was in Afghanistan our communication went from daily phone calls where he would speak to both Jamie and then me every other day, to after a very short time we would be lucky to get a two minute call a week. Eventually the chats came to all but a stop. I often ask myself if he was afraid while he was out there, though his actions didn't suggest that he was. I know he wasn't afraid to die, but I think he was worried about how Jamie and I might cope if he did.

Perhaps he was afraid of real life, and by that I mean the life he was going to have to deal with once he left the Army. Perhaps shutting off communication was his way of preparing us for what he thought was going to happen, although due to his silence I was left in the dark about it. He had promised me before he left that he'd do everything he could to stay out of danger, though I've heard since he died that that wasn't the case at all.

I found that to be a little surprising. As a species our

objective is to stay alive and survive, however, his friends have told me that he would continually go out on patrols and volunteer for anything that got him into the thick of the action; whether that was to go out to one of the forward observation posts or once there, go on a foot or vehicle patrol. I've often thought about whether any of his team knew or thought there was a problem with him. I wondered if they queried the amount of times he went out and put himself in danger, especially since he told them to keep quiet about it with me. I know if I'd seen that kind of behaviour I would have thought death would have been all but inevitable given the amount of patrols he would have put in.

Mind you, even if I had known he would most probably have ignored my fears. My ignorance of it just meant we didn't argue about it. In retrospect I think I was probably guilty of pretending everything was OK, and other than tiredness he was still his normal self. Now I look back I can see I was obviously lying to myself and everyone else. The tour had been both long and difficult, and I knew he had lost a lot of friends while he was over there. It had lasted for seven months, and the man I waved bye-bye to was not the same as the man who returned.

He was dark, moody, angry, sullen and withdrawn, and I knew he had demons inside him. He shut down and kind of communication to both Jamie and me, and while he could have his good moments, I had never seen him as angry or volatile as he had become. It has struck me since that with the number of patrols he went on, perhaps he was looking for a way out that didn't have any shame attached to it. If he'd been killed on patrol there would be no stigma, no shame, no words about not having the balls to live. In hindsight perhaps it would have suited him better to have been killed then: and I don't mean that to sound as bad as it might do.

I almost recognised the behaviour, because I too had been injured in Iraq a few years before and I had a similar feeling of emptiness as a result. I lost a really close friend in the same attack and I suffered a deep depression when I got home, though I got some excellent support, and my Flight Sergeant told me that unless I got help he would personally sign me off duty until I did. He forced me into therapy the moment he recognised I was suffering, and I am eternally grateful for him doing that. It took me a couple of months to recover, and I was in a similar place then to how I could see Chris was when he came back home. The big difference was that I did something about it while Chris let his nightmares fester. Perhaps the Army isn't as hot on mental health issues as the RAF is, I don't know.

I think becoming a parent had also changed him. Perhaps there was a little (or a lot of) guilt hidden in there too, as he had seen so many dead kids, and while his child was happy and healthy, the poor kids affected by the wars were not. Seeing dead adults is one thing, and it's expected in the theatre of war, but kids not so. This, I think, more than anything else, was what troubled him. I am naturally a talker, and as a military copper my method of trying to bring someone down from a volatile mood would be for me to talk them down, but I couldn't do that with Chris.

That made me feel pretty crappy, and I found that very difficult to deal with. In fact, it got to the time where I didn't try any more as I couldn't see the point. If I sensed an argument brewing I would walk out of the room to try and calm things down. He didn't ever follow me out to continue rowing, and so I quickly realised that was the best way of dealing with it, and while it didn't do anything constructive for our relationship, it made for a far easier life and allowed me to get on with what I had to do.

As time went on the arguments got worse and worse. They tended to come in the evening after he'd had a drink, and we argued over almost everything. Money was one of the main issues as he had his gambling problems, but in order to try and take the emphasis off what he was doing, he would deride my contribution to the marriage. At home we both had defined roles; I had taken on a part time job so that we didn't have to get a child-minder, and with my wages I bought the groceries, and at home I did the housework, looked after Jamie and the dog. I did washing, ironing and the rest of it, while Chris' only job was to pay the bills, which he continually failed to do. So while I would do all the housework and cooking; Chris would use that as an excuse to cause a tiff too.

I felt I put in a lot of effort, and it hurt because I also felt that I was completely unappreciated. What baffled me more than anything though, was his demeanour once the arguments had blown over: he would act as if nothing had happened: it may as well have been someone else having the row. There was never an apology or admittance that he had done anything wrong either, and that was even after it got physical too. Perhaps that had something to do with how he was as a man. He was a man's man and quite macho, and his idea of being strong was to never show any emotion or weakness at all. To apologise would be to admit he was wrong, and he just couldn't do that. It was a failing in him, certainly, but perhaps it was his defence mechanism. Maybe the fury was a way of him subconsciously pushing me away.

The anger in him rose at a very steady rate; so much so that I hardly even realised it was happening. After a few months of continual battling with each other I noticed there had been a change in myself too. I decided it was safer to give in rather than fight, and I found that by doing so I had become less of a person, and I was losing my own identity. The fight had gone out of me, and the last thing I wanted was an escalation of anger or violence in the home.

In 2013 Chris said he wanted to live life as a normal family and as the MoD were cutting back and shedding personnel, after a chat he said he wanted to take the opportunity and accept redundancy. When he left the Army we moved back to the UK, and up to Bishop Aukland, near Durham, and Chris got a job as a chef. He found Civvy Street very difficult to cope with, and he struggled with a daily civilian routine. He changed jobs every four or five months, and while he was never out of work – he was a firm believer in working for a living – he just couldn't get on with life outside the army. He tried to find the kind of camaraderie he had in the forces while he was in a "normal" job, but that was never going to happen.

A number of times he came home from his shift and said that he just couldn't do it, and he'd move on to the next place. We had bought a car with his redundancy settlement, and although we should have been well off financially, due to his gambling addiction it wasn't long before we ran out of cash. Then he began taking out loans to pay the household bills and keep up a normal lifestyle.

Oddly enough, we'd been married for around seven years but this was the first time we would be a normal family like everyone else. Married life in the forces is nothing like being married in any other walk of life as there is no continual day-to-day existence with your other half. You only get to see bits and pieces of them from time to time. It's almost like having a double life at times. Publicly our life was very good, though once the door shut it became a nightmare. It was horrendous. The change was gradual, and where at one time I might have argued a point here and there, at this juncture I decided not to, and I allowed things to slide in order to have an easier, quieter life. Maybe I shouldn't have done it; maybe I even enabled it?

It got to the stage where I would often have to ask my parents for money to pay our utility bills because Chris had thrown what little we had into the fruit machines. Of course, there are only so many times I could ask my mum and dad, and soon I began finding final notice letters from loan companies. His credit rating dropped to "untouchable" and so he had to go to high interest loan places and, of course, once there, you can never afford to pay them back, and so he would ignore them, and just pretend they didn't exist. I didn't find out about them for a long time because, as I mentioned, it was Chris who was supposed to look after that side of the home.

He also flatly refused to discuss the final notices that poured through the letterbox, and he still expected me to deal with the fallout from the unpaid bills and loans. His spending habits became ridiculous. He threw money at things he had no use for, or ended up with nothing to show for what he'd spent it on, and he seemed oblivious to the fact that he had to pay back the idiotic-rate-interest loans he taken out. I also found out that he had taken out a different loan against the car, which floored me. As well as his redundancy payment, he had a pension too, which was supposed to pay the bills, but that didn't happen either. As time went on he took on even more debt so that he could keep playing the slot machines.

If that wasn't difficult enough, it wasn't in the slightest bit unusual for him to get home from work and drink a slab of 24 cans of lager, one after the other. He was constantly smashed and, even now, I still struggle getting my head around how he managed to do that. Jamie was too young to understand what was wrong but he was wise enough to know how to behave around his dad. He wasn't a rowdy kid, he knew not to pester Dad, and he walked somewhat on eggshells.

We could always tell when there was a mood brewing: Chris would huff and puff, shake his head, sit down harder than was necessary, slam his cup down a little harder than usual. There were rolled eyes, looks to the ceiling and sharp exhales of breath. It was easy to see when we had to tread carefully. Jamie even began recognising the facial expressions, which is quite something when you consider he was only four years old at the time.

Small arguments got blown out of proportion and

escalated into full-scale blazing rows, and then it would get physical. There would be a slap here and a slap there, and it got progressively worse. Eventually I realised the only way to calm the situation was to walk away and go to a different room. He never followed me and that became my sanctuary. The worst thing about it was that I knew this was not the real man I married. His body was there but his mind was different and the Chris I knew was hiding in there somewhere, and more than anything, I wanted to find him again.

There was very little contact from his former army buddies either, maybe a little bit over social media, but nothing of any real substance. There was certainly no support group as such, not even a page where they might be able to chat their problems through. Odd, isn't it, that these guys trust each other with their lives when bullets are flying, but do so little for each other when they get home and try to integrate into the real world. After a lifetime in the army there's nothing to help them when they leave, yet this is the time they need it most.

At home it got to the point where there was almost nothing I could say that wouldn't send him into a rage and we would end up fighting, usually physically. The worst thing was that I never knew when or where his anger would manifest itself. There was no pattern, no triggering episodes, they just happened and blew up. By that time I had begun answering back, I had got to the end of my tether and decided I wasn't going to stand for it any longer. Big mistake. As the early arguments had ended after a single punch, they got worse. It came to a head when he grabbed me in front of Jamie, which culminated in quite a serious physical attack.

On this occasion I had asked him to take out the rubbish bins and he flipped. I knew we had come to a point where I didn't know what could happen, but this was worse than anything that had gone on before. He beat me up really badly. My face was swollen, I had two black eyes, and my arms and legs were covered in bruises. I decided I couldn't stay any longer, as I was afraid for my life. I just couldn't stay with him after that. I couldn't allow our son to be brought up in that environment and I feared for my life. I honestly believe if I'd stayed he would have killed me. That kind of anger inside a person is a horrible thing.

The last six months of our marriage we were like strangers with each other. He constantly slept on the sofa after passing out from a night of drinking. I think getting drunk helped him with the nightmares. Maybe it stopped the reality of life too. If he was constantly drunk he didn't have to face reality. I knew he was depressed, I knew he was suffering, and I knew the man I married was drowning at the bottom of a sea of lager and vodka. I begged him, and I mean literally, on my hands and knees; I begged him to get help, to see someone, anyone, not even a specialist, just someone to talk to. He said that no one else believed there was a problem, that it was only me who thought there was anything wrong, and that he didn't have any problems. He had me questioning myself and believing that it was me who was in the wrong, and that he was doing nothing out of the ordinary. After a while I stopped begging. I'd had enough.

So I left him. I took Jamie with me and we moved in with my parents and from there I looked around for accommodation in Suffolk. There was still daily contact between Jamie and Chris, as I never wanted to come between the two of them. Every child needs two parents if they can have them. After they'd chatted he would sometimes speak with me, and he was like the old Chris again, though even then there was not even the hint of an apology. Yes, he was charming, and, I have to say, in hindsight I can see he was being manipulative.

He gave me a little hope again. It even got to the point where I drove up half way to drop Jamie with him for a week's stay. I thought it would be good for them both to have a bit of "man time" together, but that went bad, as he'd got another woman to stay with him while Jamie was there, and she brought her two kids along too. That was not what I wanted or expected, and I was angry. Jamie was angry too. He felt he had to share rather than have his dad to himself, and I think after not seeing him for so long, he had a fair point. The relationship between them went to pot and Chris soon stopped contact altogether. He refused to answer any phone calls Jamie made, and that was very hard to take. I called him one day to ask if I could drive up to Durham to pick up Jamie's toys and he agreed. Oddly enough, when we spoke it was very friendly and amicable.

When we met we spoke for hours, it was a proper heart to heart chat, there were tears, which weren't angry for once, we laughed and joked, and that day he admitted to me for the first time that he was struggling and needed help. I swore to him that I would help him in any way that I could, and that whatever had gone on between him and me was water under the bridge and it could stay in the past. The most important thing for me was that Chris got healthy again and renewed his relationship with his son so that the pair of them could grow, and get to know, love and respect each other.

When we parted company that day, I felt a load that had been weighing me down for months and months had been lifted from my mind and shoulders. It felt great, and I could see a flicker of light in Chris' eyes too. I felt he had finally begun the journey back to being normal. After that we would swap the occasional one line text message here and there, but we never spoke again about him getting the help he needed. I automatically assumed he was in touch with someone and he was getting better, though I know now, of course, that wasn't the case.

By the time August came he hadn't mentioned anything about the therapy and so I asked him how it was going. My heart sank when he said he hadn't gone through with it. He said that someone had told him that people would think he was weak if he told anyone that he was struggling and seeing a shrink. It broke my heart.

We had been separated for eighteen months when I got a phone call from Chris' stepbrother. The police had contacted his mum, who in turn contacted his stepbrother and he called me and told me Chris had killed himself. I was devastated. After his death I found out he was deeper in debt than I could ever have imagined: it ran into many thousands of pounds. Had that been the final straw? Even though I knew he was ill, and even though I knew he was in debt, never, not in a million years did I ever think he would take his own life.

I never thought he would get so low that suicide would be the only option out. I felt guilt because he hadn't reached out to me, although now I understand I did everything I could have done, though I still wonder why he didn't call me that night. Jamie was devastated. Having to break that news to him, and knowing there was nothing I could do to make it better was heart breaking. There were tears, though the next day I sent him to school because I wanted him to continue with some form of normality, and I felt it would have been better to have his friends around him. I can't imagine the hurt he must have felt, though I believe it's important to be honest.

I told him that Chris had been poorly, and his head wasn't right, but still, to this day, he describes his dad as strangling himself. I'm sure he still struggles a little with it. He went through stages of anger and refused to accept it. Then he went back to sucking his thumb and wetting the bed, and if I'm late picking him up he can have a meltdown, though I have seen the other side where he tends to try and help others who are grieving or sad.

I recently found out that some of Chris' friends also suffer, and since his death a number of them have been shocked into seeking help. I still speak to a couple of his former mates and I recognise some of the traits, even though the guys may not be able to admit it admit it to themselves, or recognise it, even. I think there's a stigma attached to mental health, and there certainly is when you're working in a place that's as macho as the Army is.

Whether what Chris told me about his friend's poor advice was true or not I don't know. Of the only people who do, one is dead. What I do know is that one Sunday in November of that year, the police showed me a photo text that Chris had sent. It was a noose. The reply to the text was, "Do it, the world would be better without you in it."

We don't know how long after that it was that he killed himself. His body was found on the Tuesday after the text was sent. His boss went round to the house after Chris failed to turn up for work and discovered him when he peered through the letterbox the man saw a pair of feet hanging, and he called the police. Chris was only 44 years old. He had spent 21 years of his life giving everything for his country, and he'd been out of the army for two years.

He solved his problems the day he hung himself, although ours continue to this day. Every day Jamie misses his dad. With every day that Jamie gets older, his dad misses his achievements and him becoming a young man. Chris will never be able to watch his son grow. He will never meet any grandchildren his son might have given him, and he will never be able to enjoy any of his celebrations.

Whether Chris found peace or not we will never know. But for the sake of taking a couple of minutes to speak to someone who could have helped him he has lost everything. He left a kid wondering why, and what could have been. I beg anyone who may be reading this; if you're struggling with life, speak to someone. The alternative is devastating. If you can help someone, do so. Don't urge them to end their life, even if you think they don't mean it. That could be the thing that pushes them over the edge.

Corporal Chris Small 1972 - 2016

Three: Luke Scott, 29, Yorkshire

My early life was pretty much as normal as anyone else's. I was loved, my parents were very supportive and I had a happy enough childhood. There was no trouble at home, I was OK at school, I got on well with people and I had the usual friends who I got on with. You would never have suspected from my childhood that I would one day end up looking from the edge of a bridge thinking that I was of no worth to any of my friends or family, and that they would all be better off without me. I heard later in life that my grandparents had probably suffered from depression, but as I child I had no inkling of that. Life was good, my neighbourhood was nice and clean, my parents were together and I had no complaints.

As a kid I always dreamed of joining the army. I remember from a very early age that was what I wanted to do. I wasn't interested in becoming a fireman, an engineer or anything else. I just wanted to join the army, and so when I was sixteen I left school and had a go at the proficiency test. I passed it, joined up, and I was thrilled. I joined the Royal Electrical and Mechanical Engineers (REME) and I felt like my life was about to take off. I was living my childhood dream. I did the six weeks basic training and passed out, I was proud of myself and so happy that I was going to achieve my ambition.

The first day was all about getting my kit together, and after that it was on with Army life, which I was very much suited to. It was regimented, I had a great bunch of ready made mates and I loved the regime. Being a mechanic was also skill that could last me the whole of my life, and with good discharge papers when I got either too old or felt I'd had enough, I pretty much thought I could walk into a decent job.

I was on a basic training assault exercise in Bassingbourn one day; we'd been running all morning, and in the afternoon we had a jaunt from one part of the base to another, doing the usual stamina training, when I felt a twinge in my right knee. I thought it was something I could run off and so I continued, though the further I ran the worse it got. I was around five kilometres into the run, I was carrying a Bergen with around 25 kilos of kit on my back, I had a rifle that weighed around four or five kilos and the weight added to the problem, perhaps even caused it.

I thought back to when I was a kid and I was playing football; I guess I must have been twelve or thirteen years old at the time, and my foot twisted and my kneecap popped out but slotted back into place quickly. It hurt like hell at the time and I wondered if it was that same thing recurring. I carried on running but it got so bad that I slowed to a walk and soon I had to sit down as the pain was too much to bear. One of the Sergeants called for a lift and I was ferried back to base in an old army green Land Rover. I had a couple of days off and the swelling went down and it felt better. After a short bout of physiotherapy it went back to normal and everything was fine.

Around six months later I was in phase two of training and on anther normal PT gym session in Borden, when my knee popped again. It came out of nowhere. I hadn't twisted it or jerked it: it just popped out while I was running. It felt like twang behind my kneecap, like a ligament had snapped. When I think back, maybe I should have had an X-ray or scan but I didn't. Little did I know my dreams were about to come crashing down around my ears. I was called in to see an officer who told me I was going to be discharged on medical grounds. They'd done some digging and found my application form where I said I'd had an injury when I was a kid, and they said that as it was recurring it couldn't be put down to the Army's training that caused it. Talk about a slap in the face! I guess I shouldn't have been so honest with them when I first joined up, because I had disclosed the childhood injury, and that meant there wouldn't be a military compensation pay out. Even now I run every day, though with only my natural bodyweight to contend with, the knee holds up well enough. It still aches from time to time, though not like it did back then. It was excruciating when it happened.

I was only just eighteen years old, and my ideal life was in ruins. Everything I had dreamed of was turning to shit, and it floored me. All I had wanted to for the best part of my life was to be a soldier, and I'd put everything into that. To say I was devastated didn't come close. I left the Army and all the potential it offered in December 2009 and I went back to normal life back at home. Then another worry hit me: I had been so wrapped up in being a soldier for so long that I had never thought about a Plan B.

Back then I was hooked up with a girlfriend called Kate, who I'd been seeing for quite some time and a couple of months after my Army discharge she got pregnant. Although we both understood the risks of having unprotected sex, we hadn't planned for it and that made me feel the pressure of responsibility, and that weighed heavily on me. At around five weeks into the pregnancy Kate was in a lot of pain, and we found out it was ectopic, which meant the baby was forming in the fallopian tubes rather than the womb. It's a life-threatening situation for mum too, and it had to be dealt with by surgery. Obviously, we lost the baby.

I was a bit of a typical male initially; I thought everything happens for a reason and I didn't fully understand how it would affect Kate, or me for that matter. While I wasn't blasé, I could probably have been a little more supportive. In hindsight we weren't ready for a child but the biggest worry for us then was that with only one fallopian tube there was far less of a chance of her becoming pregnant in the future, and we both knew we wanted children.

We were both very young – I was still only eighteen – but from really early on in our relationship I always felt that there wouldn't be anyone else, and that Kate and I were meant to be together. Kate moved in with me at my mum and dad's house and things began to return to normal. Although I didn't have a job I was at college studying for a mechanics qualification, a kind of continuance from the Army's mechanical division, but the way the other students treated the teachers and staff made me feel like I didn't want to be a part of it. They were continually rude and had no respect for them or the subject they were supposed to be learning – a far cry from the Army – and after some time I left the course.

Kate was also at college and as we were both part time we spent a lot of time in each other's company, and we tended to get under each other's feet and we both got pissed off. We'd stopped seeing our friends and we were so on top of each other that it brought arguments, and it wasn't long before we were on a break, even though we still spent the odd night together here and there. It was while we were on a break, in July of 2010, when I found out she was pregnant again. Initially I didn't believe her as we had broken up only the day before, though it turned out to be true. While we were both pleased, although there was also the fear that there could be another ectopic pregnancy.

We got back together again and for a short while we carried on as we had before, though it wasn't long before we were once again arguing and breaking up on a regular basis. Even though we had our problems; Kate was hormonal and I didn't understand the changes her body and mind were going through, whenever we broke up, which was often, we still vowed we would support each other emotionally and financially even if we weren't together.

During the pregnancy we ended up back together again, but because of all the arguing we went through I didn't feel so much of a bond with my little boy, Logan, when he was born. Again there had been complications as he was born four weeks early. The day before his birth I had been out with my friends and I had a few too many drinks and ended up having a fight. The day he was born I was at Hull City's game with my dad, and at half time while I was queuing for a beer and hot-dog the hospital called me and told me Kate was in labour and close to delivering. I necked my beer and ran; hot-dog in hand, to the hospital that was only ten or so minutes away.

When I got there I put my hot-dog on the bedside table and a couple of hours later Logan was born. Considering we were on yet another break, we did quite well. I stayed at her place so that she could sleep and Logan and I could bond a little better. I saw him every weekend and once during the week and I reapplied to join the army, and once again my hopes were dashed. I appealed their decision but I lost, and so that meant I was still a civvy. Right up until I was 24 years old I thought about how things could have been had I made it. While I tried to get on with my life Kate and I were arguing more and more and on another predictable break.

As Logan was still very young and there was lots of the usual work to do with him, we didn't get much chance to grieve properly over the first pregnancy. I don't think either of us realised how much that would affect us, but it did. It was an awful time and it was down to neither of us really knowing what the other wanted that led to arguments, which got worse as time went on.

Kate's parents were not involved too much; she didn't have a great relationship with them, and her mum wasn't much of a mother figure to her. I think the way her mum was affected how Kate behaved and how she saw life and our relationship, and that didn't do us any good at all. When she became a mum herself at only 17 years old it was traumatic for her, which was in total contrast to how my parents were; solid, stable, reliable and loyal. My mum was a nurse in the NHS and she had this aura of caring about her, and so she was a big help to all of us.

Mum was also able to work flexi-time in order to

cope with the changes in all our lives and she was incredibly supportive, just as she always had been. My dad was the same too: always willing to help out. At a time I thought no one could be more supportive than they already had been, they went another mile extra, and were incredible. They never blew their tops; they would sit down and were calm and collected, and were able to address the problems and dealt with them responsibly. Mind you, as much as they told me not to worry, I couldn't stop myself from doing so. Every waking moment I was filled with dread at the thought of fatherhood.

I think that being so young and not knowing how to deal with life in general meant we did things wrong and we rowed so much that it turned into a custody battle over Logan. No one really wins in those situations, and the child usually comes off worse than everyone as one parent can get alienated, however, we were really fortunate that my parents stepped up and took custody of him. They were a huge source of help and support in a time that was rough for everyone.

Because I still lived with my parents it was almost like I had custody of him, and in time Kate saw plenty of him too. We also found a way to get past our arguments and sort out our differences. We grew to realised it was through the grief of losing our baby that we argued. My way of dealing with it was to walk away and ignore, and so the nights I was supposed to have Logan I ended up in the pub drowning my sorrows.

True to form Kate and I were having our ups and downs and we found out she was pregnant again when Logan was only 18 months old. Again she was really worried due to the first pregnancy and she was in and out of hospital quite frequently even though there were no complications. She wanted everything to be OK and I thought she was overdoing it. The doctors told us there was nothing wrong and I was as supportive as I could be even though we were on and off again, and I thought we'd be OK once the arguments stopped.

Throughout December she'd had complications and while she was in quite a lot of pain, all the scans and medical advice was that everything was OK and on course, that we had nothing to worry about and that she should relax as she was doing too much. I went to bed early on New Year's Eve as I was going to have Logan the next day, and while I was getting ready to go and pick him up I got a phone call to say Kate was in hospital. She was only 25 weeks into the pregnancy when she again had some pain and her waters had broken, so I rushed there as fast as I could to be with her.

When I got there the news wasn't as bad as I thought it was going to be, although the staff said they wanted to move her to another hospital, that had more incubators and much better equipment and if the baby was in trouble then it was the best place to be. My head was in pieces. Kate was stressed out, and where I had always been the stronger of us, as much as I could I kept a calm head but inside I was in a terrible panic. Then a doctor told us we were going to be transferred to Sheffield, and it wasn't until we got into the ambulance and they turned on the blue lights that I realised the shit was really hitting the fan. All the way there, even though I tried to put on a brave face for her sake, I could only think the worst, and I could tell she had the same thoughts too. It was scary.

We had been there for two days and while Kate was hooked up to a heart monitor we could see there were irregularities with the baby's heartbeat. It was up and down, it would hit really high beating points and then drop into a slow beat, sometimes stopping altogether. We continually called the nurses and as much as they told us there was nothing to be concerned about we were both in a state of fear. We knew that it was anything *but* OK as we'd been through similar before and we knew what a healthy heart rate should look like and sound like on the machine. This was totally different. Hours passed and still we were assured it was normal, and then the monitor signal went blank. I called a nurse who said that the baby had just turned over, but a minute or two later a team of eight doctors and nurses came into the room and performed an emergency delivery.

Kate was attached to a drip to help with contractions but it only ended up forcing them, and when the baby came out I could see he was dead. I felt numb. I walked out of the curtained area for a moment to try to gather myself and took a couple of deep breaths. I felt like I wanted to walk away but I knew I couldn't. I wanted to be strong for Kate and so I steeled myself and went back to her side. I saw a nurse cleaning blood from the baby. I couldn't believe how small he was. He was perfectly formed and he looked beautiful. I was heartbroken. My son was still. He lay there not moving, not crying. Dead. Kate was in pieces: she was an emotional wreck, and the bed was covered in blood.

The hospital staff were pretty poor, come to think of it. They left Kate on a set of bloody sheets for three hours and then they asked us to leave. She was still in pain and was in no fit state to be moved and so I kicked up a fuss. As I had come with her in the ambulance we had no transport home, and so under quite some duress they eventually allowed us to stay another night. I wondered where their compassion was.

The next day we had to vacate the bed and the staff asked us to leave our son with them, and said they would transfer his body. Due to the way we had already been treated we didn't want to do that. I called my parents and when they arrived to take us home, we put our son, Jaden, in a Moses basket. I remember looking at his tiny little body. It was the worst moment of my life.

We put him on the back seat of the car and set off back to Hull, all of us silent. I know she wasn't thinking straight at the time, but my mum mentioned about going to a McDonald's drive thru to get something to eat but my dad cut her off quickly. I'm sure it was due to the surreal situation she said it, as it was totally out of character for her. I had already spoken to the funeral directors and so we headed there and dropped little Jaden's body off.

We spent some time with him, and then went home. At the ages of 18 and 20, as parents we had to plan a funeral. I had trouble sleeping. Kate had trouble sleeping. We spent many nights crying. We were both sleeping away from each other at the time, and so we didn't have each other for comfort either.

It was a couple of months after Jaden died that matters took yet another horrible turn. I was busy at work when I saw a couple of police officers walk into the office. It wasn't long before my boss called me in and my immediate thought was that there must have been a problem with one of my family, and maybe someone had been hurt: or worse! I was nervous when I sat down with them. One of them said a woman had accused me of rape. What? He repeated it, and said someone had made an allegation that I had raped her.

I couldn't believe it. I was shocked. Horrified. I sat silent for a moment or two, and just shook my head in disbelief. I couldn't take it in. This had to be some kind of sick joke? But it wasn't. Then one of the policemen asked if I was OK and if I understood what they'd said. I nodded and asked them who it was, but they said they weren't obliged to tell me. That struck me as pretty bloody unfair, to be honest. If some woman had said I'd raped her then surely I had a right to know who she was.

I went with them to the police station and was taken

into an interview room. They asked me a couple of questions about where I'd been on a certain night, and if I remembered being with a girl. I thought back to the one-night stand I'd had with a woman in a club, and said I had, but there was no way it could have been her. She was completely up for it and was a willing and thoroughly enthusiastic participant. Then they told me that it was her, and that she said that I had raped her. I was furious by this time. I told them there and then that I had met the girl a couple of times, and on the second occasion we had sex back at her place, but it was consensual. I thought to myself I had better not say anything else until I'd spoken to a solicitor, but my world was falling apart yet again.

I was pretty angry, though the officers were actually quite good with me. I guess they had to do their job, and while I was furious with being falsely accused I understood they had to do their part too. That didn't make anything easier for me though. Once I calmed down they explained that however I felt, and whether or not I had actually done what she said I did, they had to investigate it. They asked me to go through the whole process of what had happened: how we'd met, where we went, how the night progressed, where we were, what I had been wearing, how the sex was and how we had it: everything.

I took a deep breath and told them my version of events. I'd been on a night out clubbing with my friends. We met a couple of girls in the club and decided to go back to a mate's flat and have a few more drinks. We chatted for a while and got on really well. I asked her if shed like to see me again and she aid yes. We went out the next night in Hull city centre and ended up back at her place and we had sex. I thought we were going to see each other again, but I didn't hear anything for a couple of weeks, and so she went out of my thoughts. I was embarrassed having to explain what had gone on.

I understood that the police had a job to do, and after I explained what had actually happened, I answered all of their questions as honestly as I could, and I didn't give any "no comment" replies, I was straight. They didn't treat me like I was a rapist, they were professional the whole way through and did what they could to calm me down and put my mind at ease. I had never been I trouble with the police, I had done nothing wrong that I was aware of and so while the accusation hit me hard, I have to thank them for being professional with their questioning.

That accusation turned my life upside down yet again. I was shocked. It came from totally out of the blue and I had never expected anything like it to happen. As I had only been in my job for three months or so, no one there knew me really well and I suppose it's natural for some to judge before they get the full picture. Having said that, my workmates were really supportive and they didn't treat me any differently other than being great and on my side. They knew the kind of person I was; always around for others and trying to help them out. Most people enjoyed spending time with me, and they were almost as surprised by the accusation as I was.

While I went out and got drunk in lieu of the time I was going to spend in prison, they were all very positive and told me I'd be fine. Not one of them said the otherwise; they all mentioned about the lack of any evidence, and as sure as I was that I was going down, they felt quite the opposite. Still, I had to live with the thought of going to jail for something I hadn't done; losing my freedom, being on a sex offender register, being shunned by people I knew; my friends and my family. It was a horribly low point in my life and again, I got drunk to blot it out.

The one thing that kept me focused throughout the

ordeal was my little boy, Logan. Whether it was yet another interview at the police station or going through a day at work, I wanted to prioritise my son. I wasn't making a lot of money but it was enough to make me feel like I was doing my bit and at least putting some food on the table. Even with my little lad as the focus of my life, and that I had some kind of purpose, I was depressed. I was depressed about the breakup, the fact that I couldn't provide a home on my own, and that I had been accused of a crime only one step down the scale from murder in my eyes.

Even though we were on and off, Kate was also very supportive. We were on a break and so I hadn't cheated on her. She backed me all the way and even though I had thoughts of going to prison, she was there for me. I would run scenarios through my mind, and even though I think I can handle myself, I didn't know how I would get on in prison. It was a horrible prospect. As it turned out, Kate got pregnant again, which both added to and relieved some of my worries, as there was a distraction to keep my mind occupied.

Once again we began the worrying process. Her worries were all about the baby, while mine were for both Kate and the child's. Was I going to be around for the birth and the first few years of its life? Work allowed me to take paternity leave and compassionate leave as well as a little holiday, and that helped as I could be around for Logan, who kept me occupied.

Three months later the girl dropped the rape charge. As much as I was relieved I was also furious that she could have done it in the first place. I haven't seen her since we spent the night together and I have no idea what happened to her, nor do I really care. Lots of questions went through my mind at the time, of course; how could she say that I had raped her? Why did she accuse me? Then why did she leave it so long before she withdrew the allegation? Was I cursed? Added to this, Kate was now heavily pregnant, and maybe in the back of my mind was the real possibility of another stillbirth. I was at a very low point in my life.

My first attempt at suicide ended in abject failure. I'd been out with my mates and during the night I'd begun to feel shitty. When we decided to call it a night and go home my train of thought wasn't going to bed, it was being somewhere at the bottom of the sea bed. I headed over to the Humber Bridge so that I could throw myself over the edge and never have to feel like shit again. As I made my way there I had visions of me falling and my life flashing in front of me in slow motion. I was getting closer to the bridge when I heard the toot of a horn and as I turned around I saw a police car. It pulled level with me, and the passenger window buzzed down. A young looking police officer asked if I was OK, and when I said I was fine he asked what I was doing there, and I made up some excuse that I was just out for a walk, but they were having none of it and they put me in their car.

They asked a number of times how I was as they drove me back into town, and the rest of the journey was me talking crap and demanding they let me out of the car. In the end they arrested me for being drunk and disorderly; probably due to my belligerence, and I can't blame them for that. The only thing that kept me from completely flipping was the fact that I could easily go back to the bridge and have another chance at doing myself in. I knew I would be able to do it properly, and next time I was determined I would it right. I visited the bridge on a number of occasions after that with suicide at the forefront of my mind, however, once I was there I would make a phone call to a mate and I ended up walking away, the distraction of the chat being the reason I didn't jump.

Another couple of similar occasions saw the police

pick me up again, and the same results ensued; I got a ticking off and was let out of the car in the town centre. A few months down the line and while life continued I was still suffering from some depressing thoughts. Everything got too much for me, and while I'd been feeling low for some time, I took a dive in both my self-confidence and my own worth.

It was 2017 and Christmas was around the corner. In order to distract myself and make me feel a little better about who I was, I'd been out buying presents for the family. It was traditional for us to do a secret Santa, and so I bought for my nieces and nephews, and I'd got Kate a present as we had got back together again just after the rape allegation. I did some shopping through November and mid-way to December, but I found it a struggle to go from place to place pretending everything was fine, when I knew it wasn't.

I was constantly battling demons. Although I didn't have much money, which was something else weighing heavily on my mind, I tried to make up for the fact that I wasn't going to be there by buying extra little things for the family and spending more on them. I hoped that by doing that it would be a better way for them to remember me for when I was no longer there. Christmas was just around the corner and I was going to end my life. I hadn't planned for it to happen on Christmas Day, it just went that way.

At the time I was a bus driver and I'd been working during Christmas Eve, and when I finished my shift I went home as usual, and then out with my friends having the traditional few beers with my family, and after they went home I was with friends and being the happy one amongst everyone else. None of them had any idea what I had planned, although through the drunken statements I made some of them got worried and asked if I was OK. I laughed and said that of course I was.

By that stage of the night I knew I was going to do it the next day, but I didn't tell anyone because I didn't want to ruin their festivities. Looking back now I recognise that I was a good, rich part of their lives too, but back then I couldn't see it. I felt that my mates would also be better off without me being there. It was an odd time; there I was, putting on a brave face when inside I felt like I was dying.

My mind was muddled with ideas of how I should wake up with three kids rather than two, and that it just wasn't right to do that, and that the whole family scenario of Christmas Day wasn't going to be the same.

I couldn't see what I had got: only what I hadn't. Strangely, I felt a certain amount of relief. I'd had an enjoyable night and I was going to go out on a high. It felt like a leaving party that no one but me knew it.

That made me feel even more ready to die. I couldn't get my head around how I was such a failure, or that everyone's life would be so much better without me being there. I could picture it in my head like it was crystal clear. I knew what I had to do. The only thing that made me feel even anywhere near normal was Logan, but even with him in mind, I still wanted to die.

After I left my mates I went home and had another couple of drinks. Mum and Dad were both in bed and asleep. Now it was time. There was no thought about how they would react, or how it would completely trash the period for everyone for the rest of their lives. I felt that whatever I did wasn't good enough and that I didn't deserve happiness because of what I'd been through. I wanted the pain to end.

In the times I'd been to the bridge before I'd dropped a small pebble over the edge and counted the seconds until it had disappeared from view, and I estimated it would take around five seconds for me to hit the water. I wondered what my thoughts would be while I was falling, but I couldn't think of a single thing. Nothing. As I approached the bridge I saw the driving school to my left, and just after the first of the concrete stanchions that hold the suspension cables I saw the dirty brown water of the river. Another look to my left and I could see a couple of cars parked, perhaps taking in what there was of the view, and I wondered if an of them would see me. I wandered a couple of hundred metres further along the bridge and stopped, looking out over the river. I can't have been there for more than ten minutes when I heard a shout.

A member of the bridge staff had seen me via their cameras and called the police. I'm convinced that had they not called the police I would be dead now. I'd made up my mind and I had done all the psychological preparation. A few minutes later fifteen or so police vehicles arrived, and then I saw the police helicopter buzzing around a couple of hundred feet away from me. The lifeboat was also called out. There was a team of firearms officers there too, one of whom shouted towards me that if I did anything wrong they would shoot me. I wondered if they understood that was exactly what I wanted them to do. I wanted them to pull the trigger because I didn't want to be there any more. I guess they were pretty clueless when I look back on it, but the officers who came closer and spoke to me were very different. I could tell they wanted to help. They were much calmer and friendlier and they eventually talked me down and drove me to a secure unit.

I was assessed and then taken to the police cells in Hull where I spent the best part of Christmas Day. The Christmas dinner wasn't too good either: microwaved lasagna! The good thing about the former arrest was that I could pass it off as a drunken escapade rather than a suicide attempt, which meant that no one was any the wiser. This time, however, my parents were called in and I had to face the music. My dad hugged me and there wasn't much of a conversation, just tears and relief. I didn't say much: I was embarrassed, ashamed, relieved, all of these things. While I was hugging my parents I was relieved. At last the secret was out. It was a really odd feeling. I knew they knew, and they knew I was struggling. I also felt as though I'd let them down too. So the initial relief from the negativity I felt was replaced with new negativity that I had let them down yet again. I felt shame that I could have brought my family to feel like this.

We got home and I avoided the questions as much as

I could, and of course there were raised eyebrows because I'd missed Christmas morning, and that made me feel that once again I had proved to myself that I was a failure. I'd proved everyone right: I couldn't even commit suicide properly. I was useless. After that mum and dad asked me on a daily basis if I was OK, and I guess they kept a little bit of a secret eye on me. They couldn't have done more for me.

The episode did make me rethink a few things, and that maybe this was an opportunity to get my act together and start again. I reassessed my life, started going to the gym and getting fit, and that lasted for a short time. Just when I thought everything was well with me, I sank back into depression. I don't know why, but I did. Bizarrely, the only thing that kept me going was the fact that I could have another chance at killing myself. I knew I could do it properly and next time I was determined I would it right. That would happen eleven months later.

Life continued and as well as at work, whenever I went out I always felt that people saw me as the life and soul of the party. Wherever I went I would find someone I could have a drink with. It was never anything ridiculous; just a normal social gathering here and there, but there was always drink involved. In British culture there's a certain amount of kudos for being able to handle your beer or being a beer monster, and so I just thought I was having a great time. I never thought that my drinking habits were a problem until a couple of years ago.

I wasn't the kind of guy who would wake up and think that I needed a beer, or that I had to find an excuse to have a drink, but I did make myself available for going out whenever I could. I never thought of myself as an alcoholic, but it got o the point where a couple of my friends did. There were a number of them who told me I should make an effort to go to Alcoholics Anonymous, and they said it more than once, but I didn't see that I had a problem. I couldn't think of myself as an alcoholic, I just enjoyed a drink. Then again, I suppose all alcoholic say that as an excuse to have another tipple.

I still don't honestly believe I was or am an alcoholic: I'm coming up to two years without having a drink, and I could always go really long periods of time without having a drink too. It wouldn't dwell on my mind either, I could easily go a while without even thinking about it. I just think that there were points when I was low and I did have a drink everything got worse. There were times

I would go out in order to meet people I knew would be out so I could get drunk, but I think that was more to do with the depression than needing to drink to satisfy an alcoholic craving. The bad point about that was, that that was when the suicidal thoughts came to me. I felt I wanted to end my life peacefully and with no pressure, nobody getting at me, no one to speak to. Eventually it came to the point where I was once again stood on a bridge, looking down and thinking this was the only option to end how badly I felt.

The whole journey from leaving the army to being ready to end my life was around six years. I realised I was struggling, though I didn't know how to deal with it. The first signs I recognised were the fact that if I couldn't find anyone else to have a drink with I would go to the pub on my own. There was the occasional person who would ask me how I was and I'd answer that I was fine, although I knew I wasn't I never felt like I could talk to anyone because I thought they'd see me for the failure I was, so I drank more to blot it out.

Some nights I wouldn't get home until 7 o'clock in the morning. That played havoc with my parents too, there they were looking after my kid, and there I was getting pissed rather than spending time with my son. I think mum and dad knew I needed help as they brought up the subject a number of times, but I did the stiff upper lip thing, scoffed at the mention of it, and just got on with it. Still, they were worried and I knew it, and the only way to get rid of the guilt of making them feel like that was to go out and get pissed out of my head again. Clever, eh?

When I was at my low points I would think about doing myself in again. I was in so much pain emotionally that the only way out that I could see was death. I thought everyone's life would be better without me being there. The only people I could see having a better life without me being in it was my kid, and it was only thinking about him when I stood there looking over the edge that kept me from doing it a couple of times previously. The police had picked me up around three or four times, and each time I made an excuse as to why I was there and each time I was allowed to walk free. Unless there was some kind of evidence that I was going to harm myself there's really nothing they can do.

While Kate and I were still co-parenting throughout the custody battle, I was terrified that neither of us would win and that our son would be handed over to the welfare system and that he would be taken into care. It was a horrible, terrifying thought, and it was always at the back of my mind. I don't think either of us really knew what was best for him because we still didn't know what was best for ourselves. We weren't in a situation to deal with it. With both our lives in turmoil and the amount of to-ing and fro-ing we did, Kate got pregnant again. I know this must read like something from a soap saga, and at times, believe me, it felt like it.

Our daughter was born without complications and she was healthy and beautiful, sill that wasn't enough to snap me out of an ever-deepening world of hurt and darkness. When I think of all the things I had going for me, it seems ridiculous to think I felt the way I did. That's the thing with depression though; you never know when or how you're gong to be affected by it, even when you're suffering with it.

I chose the Humber Bridge because it's quite a popular spot and it's seen some successful suicides. I thought it was the best way of doing it successfully. Since it was built in 1981 there have been over 200 successful suicide deaths. Strange isn't it, that the term for a suicide can be successful? Now it was my turn. I still don't understand why there was such a strong calling from the bridge, but there was, and I guess from the first time I had decided I was going to top myself, this was the way I would do it. It was the only way I could think of that would be relatively instant and have a painless result.

The date was November the 3rd, 2018, and as an added means of making sure I got it right this time I had put on a really heavy overcoat over the top of my jacket. The bridge's span is more than a mile wide, and so even if I did manage to survive the drop, which I didn't think I would, I would never be able to swim to the shore. I'd also brought more beer with me this time to help give me the courage to jump.

At that time I had no feelings for anyone else. Yet again I honestly thought that everyone would be better off without me being alive. Of the times I had been there previously, other than being picked up by the police I'd phoned people and spoken to them, and ended up walking away in the midst of the chat; perhaps subconsciously I had wanted to get way from the danger, who knows? That was not the case this time though. I felt so bad that I wanted to end the misery and helplessness I'd been living with for so long. This time would be the last. I'd convinced myself of that. I was wrong again. Yet again the police lifted me, and yet again they took me to the mental health unit, though this time I had a kind of epiphany, though without seeing Jesus.

I thought about my two beautiful kids, I thought about my gorgeous girlfriend, and I thought about my parents, my family and friends, and my vision was clear: I really had to try and get myself out of this destructive rut I'd found myself in. I knew that if I had asked my family for anything: money, time alone, any kind of support, they would have given it to me, but it still didn't register that I needed to ask. It was surreal when I think about it. This time I stayed in the mental health unit for five days, and the support I got from those around me was tremendous, and it made me realise that they do care, and that I mattered to them. Over the years I'd been there for them and so they wanted to be there for me. After I left the unit I again joined a gym and worked toward getting my body physically fit.

Some thought I had a problem with alcohol, and I even attended AA, though I still believe that alcoholism was not the root cause of my demons. I went more to placate everyone else rather than because I thought I had a problem with drinking. I went to a couple of meetings, though the whole religion thing got to me and I didn't want to be part of that. I'm not anti-God for anyone else, but my thoughts aren't that way inclined. At AA, one of the twelve steps is to acknowledge that God can help you, and while I understand it brings a lot of comfort to many who climb the steps, it's not me.

No one understood how I felt. Nobody had any idea how depressed I was. I kept it from them because I knew how hurt they would be, yet I had still convinced myself they would be better off if I were dead, whereas really, I can see now I was blotting life out. Another incredible thing was that through all the arguments, all the battles and all the turmoil between Kate and me, we still loved each other. I guess we were too young to see that at the time. At the end of all of it, we got back together and we recently got married: proof that there can be happy endings to even the most horrible of stories.

Logan still doesn't know the full extent of how low I was or what I was going to do or the effect it may have on the rest of my family, and I am grateful he hasn't grown up with his dad's suicide on his mind. Now I try to raise awareness for other people in the position I was in to see there is another option to suicide.

It wasn't until years later that I realised that having to leave the Army was the trigger for my depression. I remember Steve Jobs said something about joining the dots up backwards, and by doing that I can see that's where it all began. Even up to only six months ago – I'm 29 years old now – I still had regrets about the Army and where my career could have gone. I had friends that I'd joined up with who had gone on operational tours and I wanted that. I wanted that to be me. There wasn't a day that went past that I didn't think about the Army. I felt regret every single day since I left.

I also lost some of my friends while they were fighting in Afghanistan and Iraq, and there was guilt that I wasn't there to help them, or that I couldn't do anything. I couldn't go and pay my respects at their funerals, as I didn't have the money to go and see them laid to rest. It made me feel terrible; like I was a fraud, and that I shouldn't be at home while they were risking their lives. Those feelings had built up over the years, and while I couldn't see it then, they added to the weight of depression I felt.

I still get down days, though they're not so frequent, and I accept them. I don't try to bury them any more. I can still be fun and the life of the party, but I don't feel like I need to be any more. I've been tee-total for almost two years and I don't feel like I have to perform if I feel low. I can tell people how I feel without any guilt or shame. There are certain dates that trigger the low points: the anniversary of my second son's stillbirth at Christmas time is a big one for obvious reasons. It hurts also when I hear about other people having babies as early as ours and surviving. I don't feel envious, but for me I still question why it was that our baby died.

When I feel low these days I understand that tomorrow is going to be better and I won't always feel depressed. I never hide how I feel, I tell my wife and parents or whoever I'm with. I've got a massive support system, and even though my friends might be busy they always get back to me if I call them to say that I need a chat. That is an enormous help. People look at you differently when they know you suffer with depression. Perhaps that's because there's still a stigma attaché to it and it's still relatively taboo.

Medication helps but there are other ways to help before it gets to that stage. As I have mentioned, I was fine up until I left the army. It was only when I lost that sense of being what I wanted to be and contributing to an outfit, an organisation or the country that I began feeling bad. Depression is an invisible killer. The process of recovery is about being open to the truth, being open to talking to people about how you feel. It wasn't massively difficult for me as the police had already told my folks I was going to jump off the bridge, and so they knew there was a problem. That made it easier for me to come out with the truth. These days I'm on medication and have been since the last attempt. I take 100 milligrams on Sertraline a day and that keeps me stable. The one problem with medication is when people stop taking it.

From my recovery and the support from my November 2018 attempt and a short stay in a mental health assessment unit I was directed to a care coordinator in my community mental health team and I saw my counsellor weekly. I'd heard about fit mind and fit body, and so I decided I would join a gym and get some exercise, which might take the darker thoughts out of my head. I focused more on my job and my family, and slowly things got better. My counsellor also directed me towards a couple of support groups and one of them was a local recovery college group all about mental health and well-being. They had a couple of courses and one of them was boxing, which I had always had a keen interest in.

I went there every Thursday and that developed into

going to some evening sessions too. I remember one night I was going home and my body ached like hell, and a part of me questioned why in God's name I would do this to myself, but it felt good. It felt like I was alive and able to achieve something in life. It made me want to carry on. I thought to myself, we go again tomorrow, and that became my mantra. I told myself time and time again: "We go again. We go again." If I woke up in the morning and felt crappy, I'd say it again. If I felt low at some point, I'd say it again.

It got to the stage that I began helping out with the boxing sessions and I became a bit of a motivator for some of the youngsters. Slowly as I reflected I realised that I was using the term "we go again" a lot. When I broke it down and why I used it, it inspired me. I set up a YouTube channel to see if my story might help other people who had been in similar situations, and from there it became a business.

It's more than a brand name, it's also a mind set. When the chips are down we don't give up, we go again. It's come from my struggles to helping others, and it's also an opportunity to educate people and try to help others deal with what they're going through. As I was doing so many nights and so much for other charities I decided the best bet was to start a business. I could still contribute in other ways to the five charities I carry out volunteer work for. The main reason for doing it as a business rather than a charity was so that I could give back and help those who had supported me, and there were so many that a single charity wouldn't cover it. It means I can sponsor teams or people and give more support that way.

The reason I set up *We Go Again*, was to help people in the same situation as I was in. Sometimes when I speak to people about how I felt and that I wanted to kill myself and I might smile about it, they look at me as though to say, "What have you got to smile about, that's nothing to be proud of?" but it's not that I'm proud of it, it's because I got through it and I can look back and smile that I'm still here. I suppose there's a certain amount of gallows humour about it too. Without having gone through that experience I wouldn't be able to help people like I do.

I don't tend to suffer so much with survivor guilt these days. Once I was diagnosed with depression and anxiety, and having the family group hug at the police station, I felt I had got a reason to be alive and that what had happened to me was a medical issue. That's why I felt and acted like I did. I still have to remind myself at times when I feel great that I can laugh without the fear that it is going to end in tears. Nowadays the low points don't last long, whereas before they could be with me for four or five days, sometimes even longer. I understand I don't have to force myself to be happy.

The recovery stage is all about accepting that life has ups and downs and as a depressive mine might be lower than other people's but that I can still get through them and not feel guilty about it. The most guilt I feel now is when I find out someone else has been successful in their bid for suicide. It's a strange expression, it's a contradiction in terms, or an oxymoron – successful suicide. I also feel that I would rather it was me than all the other people. I feel guilt that I couldn't save them, though I know it isn't as simple as that, of course.

Warning signs are not easy to spot. Even after I had been diagnosed the first time, I still felt that I still wanted to die. I was at a charity event a while ago, and as usual, being the life and soul but feeling miserable, and no one asked how I felt because I looked like I was having fun. Someone can go out of their house smiling and they seem like they haven't got a care in the world, and they jump off a bridge, or put a hosepipe from their exhaust into their car, or swallow a bottle of pills and alcohol, or cut their wrists, and people will say, "But he seemed so happy when he went out." That's even people who know their friends, wives, husbands, brothers or kids are depressive. I was always good at covering my warning signs with a smile or a joke. I guess it's difficult to judge.

Kate struggled with it big time. We never really had the discussions we should have had over our baby dying. Neither of us had an in-depth chat about it. She is also depressed and anxious. I can spot her warning signs: failing to take meds, comments here and there. Some people stop taking medicine because they feel better, and while it takes only a couple of days for it to stop having an effect, and then depression setting in again, it can take four or five weeks to start to make a difference, so when you stop for two days, you're down and then there's a long way back to normality. It's tough, but it's doable, and we have to be constantly aware of ourselves.

Luke Scott, 29, Yorkshire

Four: Lakshmi Khan, 22, India

I spent the first fourteen years of my life in India living with my grandparents, as my mum and dad were working in another country. I saw my dad occasionally when he visited for the odd month or two, but he was never really with me when I was a kid. I lived an almost normal life, though it was not completely without trauma. When I was eight years old a number of my uncles and one of the family's close friends began abusing me.

I grew up thinking of and calling these men uncles. They were men on my father's side of the family, and for the next five years each of them sexually molested me. As far as I know, none of them knew that the other was doing the same, though I could be wrong. They were all very different in their personality, and none would speak to the other while I was in their company. They would each use the same type of tactic to get me on my own; they would come to the house and say to my grandmother, "I'm going to take Lakshmi out to the park and get her chocolates," and my grandmother would think they were being kind-hearted, and so she would let me go with them. I don't believe she knew what they did to me while I was with them.

They took me away from the house to secluded areas and then start touching me. I cried but it made no difference to them, they continued to take what they wanted from me. I often looked around to see if I could shout to anyone who could help me, but there never was anyone there. After they had done what they wanted to do they took me home. The experience made me very fearful of men, and I avoided them as much as I could without making it obvious, so that there would be no questions asked and no repercussions that would bring shame on the family or me.

I realise now that saying nothing only perpetuates this kind of behaviour, but as a child I knew it would be their word against mine; and no adult would believe a child, and certainly not the word of a little girl. It was a horrible situation for me, and I can still vividly remember everything that happened. Since I have grown up my aunt has mentioned on a number of occasions that I was very mature for a child, but I wasn't mature. I was abused.

I still see these people and they act as though they have done nothing wrong. They come up to me and say, "Hi, what's up?" It's like they pretend their abuse never happened. I don't feel like I ever want to face them after what they did to me. I have never told anyone about this before. Not my mother, my grandmother, my aunts: no one.

Men taking advantage of me was a large part of my life until I moved away from India. I try to forget but again, at family reunions, weddings, funerals and such like, I still see these animals. They make me want to vomit when I see them, though for the sake of the family I also have to pretend that nothing happened, and act like I have forgotten. But I haven't. I often find myself asking what kind of existence is this? To this day, when a man raises his voice I get nervous.

My mum also went through a lot of trauma at the hands of her in-laws. It's a strange thing in India, that even though there are lots of cousin marriages, and the aunt and uncle become fathers- and mothers-in-law, they abuse their nieces and use them as skivvies and emotional punch bags. I have no idea why, but it seems to perpetuate and pass from one generation to the next, and they don't learn from each other that the pain they had been put through is the same pain as they are now heaping on their relatives. I find it disgusting.

When I was in Year 10 at school – so I would have been 13 or fourteen years old – my dad came back for around six months. I had been at a Swedish school for around ten or eleven years when I had to move to an Indian school because British exam boards were not recognised there. The teaching and learning styles of each of the schools were very different and it impacted on me.

I also found the Indian teachers a little odd, because rather than giving us academic guidance, many of them asked about our home and social lives and which guys had we met. It was not only me they asked, but all of the girls. I often didn't know what to say. This is a really taboo subject in India, and I think the teachers wanted to know so that they could tell our parents. In my community most daughters got beaten up at home, and plenty of us had a hard time from teachers, many whom I felt knew what was happening to me while I wasn't at school.

I went into class one day with my face bruised and swollen from a beating I had taken from my father. I looked like I had stepped out of a car crash, and it seemed as though the whole school came to have a look at me. The fact that I had to go through that for six months was embarrassing. What is worse when I look back is that no one passed comment or asked questions.

I had a friend I was really connected with and he was male and so that caused me many problems. It wasn't a relationship as such because I was far too young for any of that, but I felt a lot for him. Perhaps in my on small way I was rebelling, but I don't know. I'm not a psychologist. When my dad found out he waited for me to leave school and while I was walking along with this boy, my dad grabbed us and beat both of us up. He dragged me to the floor and punched me in the face. It wasn't a small punch, but that of a grown man fighting another man. I heard my jaw break from one of the punches. Then he hit the boy in the face too.

It was a terrible beating, but I think what hurt more than anything was the psychological effect it had on me. The attack took place in front of lots of my school friends and while I screamed in pain, I also screamed in embarrassment for my friend, for me, and also for my dad. It was so violent, and I couldn't understand how he could do this to me when it was such an innocent friendship. I remember feeling shame and thinking to myself that I have to walk this route and face these people every day, and the humiliation of getting beaten up by my parent while the whole school looked on was terrible.

There were times I simply couldn't face school because I was in so much pain both emotionally and physically, and this period of beatings lasted for the whole of the six months my dad was home.

Then he stopped me from going to school completely. He told me I would not set out of the house again. It was a terrible blow. As well as the respite it gave me from having to be anywhere near him, I loved going to school and learning, I really enjoyed it and so to have that taken from me was awful. Occasionally, when he was in a benevolent mood he would let me go, although he would meet me at the school gates and on the way home he would tell everyone we met how bad a daughter I was. The ignominy was awful. Other than the odd day at school I wasn't allowed out of my room.

He would often hit me for no reason, and when I say this I mean he couldn't even be bothered to find one of his petty excuses. I never knew what was coming at me or when. Or why for that matter! He locked the door to my bedroom and his eyes were on me constantly. Before he came to India for those six months I loved my dad. I had this picture of him being the hero and provider, but that changed when I found out what he was really like: his real personality. After that I hated him.

In some religious communities in India – certainly where I am from – when a girl is stopped from going to school and studying, people start talking about you and you are found laden with guilt just because you are no longer part of the crowd or part of that enclave of society. What hurt me more was that instead of supporting and having faith in me, my dad accused me of wrongdoing and punished me for something that was entirely innocent. He also began talking to other people about me and telling them I was no good and that I had brought shame on the family name. I had no fatherly support. For the next six months life entailed sporadic beatings and slaps from my dad. What made matters worse was that my younger brother was so influenced by my dad's behaviour and what he told him about how women should be treated, that he became like a spy for my dad, and told him everything I did, no matter how insignificant it may have been. When my dad hit me my brother thought that was how life is. Girls aren't allowed male friends! If ever my brother saw me with anyone he would snitch and I got an extra beating.

Occasionally I told my grandmother about it, and she would try to speak to my dad and stop the attacks, but instead he got worse. He had a metal rod that he would hit me with across my back, and he would hit me so hard my face would blow up like a balloon. I often found myself crying while he was hitting me and shrieking in pain. I even tried saying that I was his daughter, and that what he was doing was wrong, telling him he was hurting me, but it made no difference and the beatings continued.

I often wondered if my mother was coming in for the same treatment while he was with her in Dubai. On the few occasions I managed to speak to her I told her what he was doing and she told me to write her a letter detailing everything that was going on so that she could get custody of my siblings and me. I would cry to her on the phone but that only made her feel more helpless that she couldn't do anything to alter the situation. She would sob, apologise on his behalf, and tell me there was nothing she could do. In the end I stopped crying and just accepted it as part of life.

I had very little contact with her at this stage as my dad kept control of all communications between us. Around that time my brother was going off the rails a little, and my grandmother spoke to my mum and asked her to come back to India. She gave a month's notice to her employer and then left everything to come back.

Thankfully when she arrived things got a little, though not altogether better.

There was an occasion, I was around thirteen years old at the time, that my dad took me out of town to meet one of his friends. He told me that everything was going to be fine, and I remember thinking it was an odd thing to say. We went to a hill station that was way out of the city and I had no idea why or where we were going. When we got there he took me up to the roof of the building and as we went up the stairs he told me I should not mention anything about the beatings he gave me or the reason he got so mad and beat up my friend and me. When we got to the roof I saw another man standing there: my father said the man was his friend.

The man came to me and said I should forget my studies and go and work for him. He said he was going to take me anyway, that he had worked out a deal with my dad and so studying was pointless. A deal? I didn't know what to do. I wasn't so naïve as to not know entirely what was going on.

Once again I was terrified. I had no phone; no way of communicating with anyone. My dad was a huge man, I couldn't fight him or push against his will. His friend stood next to me and caressed my hair. He told me not to worry, that nothing bad was going to happen. He told me the deal had been arranged, and that soon I would be with him. Then his hands wandered onto my breasts and then down between my legs. I cried and he pulled his hand away, but said it was OK, because when I fail tenth grade he would come and get me and that I would work for him and be with him. Again, he told me that it was already arranged. It was then it dawned on me that my own father had made a deal to sell me to this man. I looked at my dad and told him that his guy said he was going to take me away, and all my dad did was to ask if I wanted a drink. I was shocked.

He offered me a bottle – I could see it was alcohol – and I knew it was wrong for me to drink it. In Islam alcohol is forbidden – it's haram – and I didn't want to drink. I said to him that I was only thirteen years old and that I didn't want to, but he kept telling me to, "just taste it. Try it". My dad was a big man, I wouldn't have been able to tell him "no", or run from him, that simply wasn't an option. After the beatings he had given me I truly believed that he was capable of throwing me off the roof if I didn't do as he said. I was terrified. He forced me to take a drink and so reluctantly I took a sip from the bottle.

It tasted awful and I told him I didn't like it, but he told me to be quiet and made me drink more. He forced me to drink a whole bottle and it wasn't long before I made my way to the bathroom and vomited. After I was sick I went back into the room and collapsed on the floor. I felt him pick me up and lay me out on the bed. I don't know what happened afterwards as I passed out, but I remember when I woke up the morning after my dad asked me if I remembered anything about the previous night, and I said I only remember being sick after drinking. He told me I had done lots of very bad things but he wouldn't tell me what I had allegedly done, only telling me not to worry about it. To this day I still don't know what went on.

Later on in the day the man spoke to me and told me that he was my friend and that I could tell him anything. My dad had already forbidden me to say anything about having a male friend, but I thought that even though this man was friendly enough, if anything could discourage his advances, then this might be the thing, and so I told him. He then told my dad what I had said.

We went home and later that night my dad came to my room and he was angry, saying he had told me a hundred times not to say anything about this boy, and that I hadn't listened. He slapped me hard across my face and said because of me he had been shamed. As far as my family was concerned, they believed the time I spent with my dad that day was just the two of us getting some dad and daughter time, but soon my relatives began asking where he had taken me and what had happened. My father told the family that there was only a business deal going on, however, whatever it was that was supposed to have happened didn't.

My grandfather would occasionally stand up for me, and tell my dad that he had never been there for us; that we had had no guidance or support from him, and that he had no right to stop me from going to school, and as adamant as my dad was that I should not go, my granddad took me to school on the day of my board exams. Against all odds I passed. I couldn't believe it. My grandmother and grandfather were so pleased they cried. When I called my dad I was so excited and I thought he would be too, but he wasn't, he told me he was sitting with his friend, who then spoke to me briefly and said he was disappointed because I was meant to be "for him", and that, he "really wanted me." At a time when I was supposed to be happy that I could continue my schooling, I felt bad because I had let my dad down.

The deal between him and the man collapsed.

After many of the beatings I would sit on my bed sobbing and thinking that I would be better off if I were dead. I would go up to the roof of the house and sit on the edge, two stories up, and think to myself that it would be so easy to just fall off and end the suffering. Suicide was constantly on my mind. I wanted to get out of the situation and I couldn't see any other way around it. I also thought about cutting my wrists and bleeding to death. I had heard it was relatively painless after the initial cut. I thought about hanging myself too. I still don't know what stopped me from doing it. I think it was because I didn't want to let my mother down and leave her with nothing.

After going through abuse from my relatives and that family *fiend* (I meant to say that), and then thinking about how badly my father treated me I felt only pain. It was such an awful time of my life. I could never have imagined that I would have to live a life like that with my own father being so vicious and violent towards me. Perhaps it was because he was an alcoholic that he behaved the way he did. I certainly think that made him even more irrational than he may otherwise have been. But, of course it wasn't only him. There were also the three uncles and the family *fiend* who abused me too. The question I asked myself so often was, why me? What had I done to deserve this kind of treatment from my own father? Even now I sometimes wonder how I got through it all.

One night my dad woke me and hugged me, and admitted that he had beaten and treated me like a dog. He apologised and cried. Even after all he had done I thought to myself that he is still my father, and that maybe he had finally realised that what he had done to me was wrong. I asked him the next day if he remembered what he had said because I wasn't sure if I had dreamt it, but he said he did and he said he meant every word of it. I forgave him and over the next week or so our relationship got better. He even allowed me to explain that at some point I would find love, but whatever happened I would never run away from him. He said he understood.

One morning when my brother and I were getting ready for school, my young cousin, who was around six years old and also lived with us, went to say goodbye to my dad, and when he stepped into the bedroom he saw my dad hanging there. He didn't know what to do and so he ran to my grandmother and told her that Daddy (he called him Daddy too) is joking, come and see. My gran woke my brother up and asked him to check on my Dad, and when he entered the room he let out a scream, which brought us all running.

When I stepped through the door I saw my father hanging there. His feet were no more than ten centimetres off the floor and he had his belt around his neck that was tied around a beam on the ceiling. It was obvious he was dead. It was a horrible sight. All three of his kids were there: my brother was 13, my sister was nine, I was 14, and my dad was just hanging. I can still see the image in my head. My brother had to fetch a knife and cut through the belt to get him down.

Even though he had been so violent towards me for so long, in my innocence and after his begging for forgiveness, or realisation that he had done me wrong, I wanted him to be the father that he had never managed to be. Just as I was building up a relationship with him, just after his apologies and some kind of normal life between us he killed himself.

I still have no idea why, maybe guilt, maybe depression. Perhaps it was shame that drove him to it, but I don't think so. It was probably a mixture of a lot of things, I don't know but he had tried to mend his relationship with me, and so when he died I was upset.

After my dad killed himself, his cousin, whom we called Uncle – he was married to my dad's youngest sister (it is quite normal in our society for cousins to marry) – offered my mum and my siblings a chance to start a new life. He was a wealthy man who ran his own business and so after the trauma of neglect, abuse and suicide we were happy to move away from India to a new life in another country. My uncle said he would provide for us, help with our education and see that we were all looked after, and it was with happiness we left the past behind and looked forward to a new beginning.

When we got there my brother and I began school in a CBSE curriculum whereas we were used to the British IGCSE curriculum, and we struggled. We both found it so difficult that eventually we had to leave the school, and we transferred to an Indian school but I felt there was more focus on what students did after school than during class times. Again, the teachers seemed more interested in who was in a relationship with whom, or what kind of mischief the pupils might be getting into rather than how their education was going.

At the new school my music teacher took an interest in me and before long he began writing letters to me, which quickly became romantic. He was a young man, and he said he had fallen in love with me. I didn't want this kind of attention and so I thought the way to deal with it would be to speak to the school principal. I did so, handing over the letters the teacher had sent, but the reaction was not the one I had expected.

My uncle and aunt were called and the principal told them I had been misbehaving, that I was bad, and that they no longer wanted me in the school. Then he took the letters and tore them to pieces while we watched. I stood there in shock. I hadn't written the letters; that was the teacher, yet there I was being blamed for the situation. My uncle and aunt chose to believe the school rather than me. That's when the mental abuse began.

There was a family friend teaching at my school; she knew our uncle quite well, and she gave my brother and me a really hard time. She did nothing but bad mouth us and there seemed to be trouble upon trouble heaped upon us. It was like living in hell. The teacher was friendly towards my uncle and he told us we had to respect her all the time, and so there was nothing we could say against her. She was untouchable. This woman even spat in my face on one occasion, and she would taunt us for not having a father. The only solace my brother and I had would be to pour our hearts out to each other. Neither of us was allowed a phone or to use the Internet, and my mother wasn't allowed to work outside the house. It was horrendous.

Then my uncle pulled us out of school and said he would home school us but that never happened. He told us off and said he'd stopped our education because we weren't studying, but that wasn't the case at all. We had tried really hard but with the teacher incident and the change in the system it didn't work well for my brother or me. The gap in my schooling lasted for two years, and then my uncle had someone his wife knew "a friendly teacher" come round to give us classes but we learnt little.

She was more interested in telling him about who we socialised with: boys, when in fact it was girls and boys, and all of it was very innocent. Just when I thought our lives would get a little better it seemed as though it would carry on as it had before. This time it wasn't physical beatings, but there was a lot of mental torture for all of us, my mum included. We weren't allowed to socialise outside; we were allowed no friends, no trips out, nothing. The house we were in was quite a big villa, and so my uncle used my mum as a maid. He told the rest of the family he was taking care of us though all the time he used us like free labour. We became his servants.

My mum would cook for everyone who visited the house and even though some of them were our own family we were continually looked down upon. After two years of no proper schooling out of the blue my uncle enrolled us in British Council A-Level exams, and of course, it was no surprise that we failed. Then he got mad at us for failing! He threw the cost of the exams at us, and said we were useless. How he expected us to pass A-Levels when we had zero schooling I don't know.

Then I saw an advert for a foundation unit at one of the universities, which was an off-shore, Australian university campus, and although he baulked at the idea of throwing even more money away, after my brother pleaded with him and reminded him of his promise to look after us, and after a lot of grovelling from us and soul searching from him we managed to get enrolled. The course was at a proper university, and it lasted only six months but at least it would give us some kind of coaching, and at the end there would be a certificate that would allow us to go to university full-time.

I spoke to my mum quite a lot about trying to find someone she could marry to get us out of the situation, which wasn't easy. However, one of the other maids was in touch with a man from Sudan who was a decent person and she got in touch with him. He turned out to be a proper human and he was ready to take us on as his family, and that was the beginning of our lives turning around. He made us feel wanted, and like we were people rather than objects, however, there was still the problem of my uncle being my mother's and our guardian.

After a rare phone call to my grandmother, she advised my mum to file a police complaint against my uncle. She did so and the police came the next day, though they said it was a family problem and they couldn't intervene. My uncle and aunt called my mum all sorts of names, a prostitute, slut, a fallen woman: lots of those awful terms. Even though the rest of the family knew how we were being treated they sided with my uncle in front of the police. The Asian family structure is a strange thing, and keeping "face" is something they see as important. I think perhaps it was this that made them let us down, though I cannot be certain, but as soon as my mum left for India my uncle changed. He took care of us and paid for the second term of my foundation year.

While this was going on I further encouraged my mum to find a new husband and eventually one of the other maids from told her about a man who was looking for another wife. He spoke with her on the phone a number of times and eventually they fell in love and got married. This signalled the end of living with my uncle, and the beginnings of a new, normal life.

Where my mother gets her patience from I don't know. I think it's her faith. Her new husband treats my bother, sister and me like his own children and he is an amazing man. He is like an angel to us. He has eight children from a previous marriage and he treats every one of us as equals. The rest of our family's attitude towards us also changed, and even now, when I think about how their attitudes towards us were, I am completely baffled.

I rarely think about my dad now. I have thought during this process of speaking with Andy, the author, whether I miss him or not and I can say with all honesty that I don't. Some of my friends have said they feel sorry for me but the last thing I want from anyone is pity. I am fine and I have a future to look forward to.

I hope people can read my story and see how I have come through the other side. I read about youngsters taking their lives because of exam stress and I just don't understand it. For my life to have been in such turmoil for so long during those formative years was awful, and while I contemplated suicide on many, many occasions, I always knew that death would not be the answer for me.

I'm getting married soon although my fiancé knows little about my previous life history. I have never told this story before. The reason I'm talking about it now is to express my feelings and try to help other people realise that there is light at the end of the tunnel, and that suicide is not the answer. Even for me, at the end of the day there is always hope.

Lakshmi Khan, 22, India.

Five: Mark Dale, 43, Essex

My childhood was fine, it was as normal or average as anyone else's, I'm sure. The one thing that may have been different is that my mum was poorly, but I don't think it had any great effect. She went in and out of hospital from time to time, but dad was always there. He worked a lot but that didn't encroach on how we lived. We were always well provided for, school was fine, if there were a few ups and downs, but again, nothing terrible or troublesome.

We were always taught we should try to win, it wasn't like the participation medal thing there is now, or anything like that. It was old school and it was fine. I was one of the last few kids who did O Levels before they changed to GCSEs, but again, there was nothing untoward or unusual about my school life. There was never any pressure from my family to be someone, it was just a case of do what you want to do and what makes you happy. There were no underlying issues at all.

I left school on Friday the15th of July of 1988, and on Monday morning I began working with my dad in his construction business. My long-term goal was to go to college and do something with my life and so the job with Dad was only meant to be for the summer, but I loved it. It was a fantastic experience because although I loved having my nose in a book, this was something I hadn't experienced before, I loved the banter with the rest of the guys: everyone took the piss out of each other and it was worthwhile graft. I felt like we were doing something good.

Then it came time to start college but after I enrolled I didn't get on with it at all. I thought it would be a step up from school but I found it worse. Although we didn't have teachers telling us off I really couldn't get on with it. In fact I hated it. I longed for the camaraderie with the guys I had grafted with, and even though I tried to make college work – I gave it six or seven months – it got me down. I ended up asking my dad if I could go back to work with him but by then there were no opportunities open.

Like my dad, my mum was also pretty old fashioned, and she brought us up to understand that you pull your weight in life and that you don't get a free ride, which meant I had to get a job, and, of course I agreed wholeheartedly. I got a job with a delivery firm working in the office and I liked it so much that I stayed there for 12 years! There were good days and bad days but that was work, it was life and we were treated really well by our management and customers. Come Christmas time we'd get turkeys and hampers and lots of other little gifts from clients, and I honestly loved it. Life was good. When I think about it that was easy too. I loved my work so much that my personal life went out of the window. I went to work, I worked, I went home, ate, watched a bit of telly and then went to bed to get ready for the next day's graft. I guess I could have been described as a little bit boring.

Then mum took a turn for the worse and she deteriorated quite quickly during the time I was at work. The doctors tried new medicine and treatments and even though she was relatively young; only coming up to her 50th birthday, I think her illness aged her and made her weaker. Her kidneys were giving way and the whole family could see she wasn't the person she was, and while she was on dialysis she got the offer of a transplant. It was successful and for the next couple for years she was, fine, but she eventually lost her battle in 1998. That was a shock.

Losing someone who had always been there was traumatic. My brothers and sisters were all married and had their own lives and so they had been out of the equation for some time, and at home it became just dad and me. Mum's death hit him really hard and in time I kind of became Mum, or at least took her role on by looking after him, and with that, as well as work, it began draining me. All the time I was at home I thought about work, and all the time I was at work I thought about him. My head was all over the place and I felt life was becoming less manageable and also less enjoyable.

Recognising how things went bad isn't easy. At the time I remember seeing little things that became different than the norm. The depression would hit me in waves and at different times, mainly while I lay in bed and had time to think. I would sometimes surprise myself by remembering the things I used to do. I'd think, to myself that I don't do this or that any more, and I noticed I was losing little pieces of myself. There were things I recognised that I didn't want to do anymore too. Things that made me who I was, and I couldn't think why I didn't want to do them.

These thoughts would hit me now and again after weeks or months, and I would question myself and ask myself, "What am I doing with my life?" Not only was it becoming less manageable, but it was also becoming less enjoyable. It wasn't only the mental side of things either, I felt weak in my body as well as my mind. I found myself taking days off work and making excuses for why I was AWOL. I would sleep for as long as I possibly could; waking up and feeling drained and forcing myself back to sleep so that I didn't have to face getting out of bed.

The amount of excuses I went through fobbing my employers off was ridiculous. It was anything I could think of and in the end I ran out of new things to say. It got to the point where they told me that it couldn't go on, and if I'm honest, they took a long time to get there. I think lots of other employers would have fired me long before that, although at the time I couldn't give a shit what they, or anyone else thought. From my point of view the best thing they could have done for me would have been to fire me. It would have made not having to lie to them and make excuses easier. Work, though, was the least of my worries. Nothing was enjoyable. Everything seemed dead.

I knew that something was wrong but I didn't know what it was or why. I had resigned myself to feeling like that, and Dad mentioned a couple of times that I should see a doctor but I couldn't see how a GP would help with how I felt. If I didn't know how I felt, how would a doctor know? I couldn't describe how I felt to anyone, myself included. I just didn't know. This was round about the end of 1999 and the start of 2000.

The whole process was like something slowly eating at me from the inside of my head, there was no quick crumble. I think there was a Monday morning blues beginning, and it got gradually worse and worse. Shamefully I used the excuse of my family to get out of work, and when I did manage to get into the office I walked around like I was a zombie. I had become a husk of the man I used to be. One of my colleagues mentioned that he'd seen me the day before and although he called out to me a number of times, he said it was like I was deaf.

This behaviour, or feeling, went on for around a year and I got worse and worse, and while my head was up my arse, my dad also took ill. This was around the end of 2001, and he was diagnosed with acute myeloid leukemia, which meant the prognosis was terminal and that his death would happen soon. The doctors said while they could keep him comfortable, his standard of life would deteriorate very quickly. I went into autopilot and became a nursemaid, being there for him when he needed me. I didn't feel any emotion at the time because of this robot mode I had gone into.

Whether that was a coping mechanism I don't know, but I was dead to having any feelings. The routine for us became a three-times weekly visit to the hospital for a blood transfusion, and he'd be a little bit better for a day or so, and then he'd get weak again until the next blood swap. It was a horrible thing to have to watch day after day, and I'm sure even worse to have to endure. Although he knew he was going to die, Dad was a strong old boy. He wasn't ever a glass half full guy, and even if the level f the cup did get lower, he was the kind of man who would tip it into another, smaller cup, so that it would be full again. He was a very tough cookie.

Because I lived with him, I was Dad's natural carer. My siblings did what they could but as they were scattered far and wide they weren't in a position to help that much, They did take him and look after him for the occasional day or two, which helped, but when he was away I had only my own thoughts to deal with, and they were getting darker by the day. While he was with me I had a focus, when he was away there was emptiness.

None of my family knew how I felt. I used to put on Oscar-worthy performances when they came round to visit, and they would never have guessed how I was crumbling inside. I was still battling in my own head with how I felt, and so the last thing I wanted was to discuss my feelings with someone else. I smiled, I laughed, I joked and I made cups of tea. I also think that because they had their own families and problems to deal with, that I didn't want to burden them with how I was, and while I already felt dead inside, I wasn't about to heap that upon them, and the last person I wanted to tell was Dad! How could I, given what he was going through?

I had friends but few whom I could really chat with, and although there was one mate I was close to, when I did see him I had the mask on then too. I was cold inside. He was good though. I think he saw I was struggling, though whenever he asked me any tough questions, or if he got close to the problem I would push him away.

As much as I'm sure he could probably see I was really struggling I still didn't want to admit it to myself. Whenever he broached it I would change the subject; even now he still looks out for me and asks me how I'm doing, bless him.

When Dad died I don't think it hit me as hard as it did with my mum. I'd had more time to understand and realise he wouldn't be here for much longer, and so there was no shock. It sounds awful but it's true. With my mum, she'd been ill throughout my life, almost, but with dad it was very quick, and although I'd had prior warning, I still felt that he could get through it and beat it. I really did, and that was right up until the end.

As it was, he didn't die from the disease he was suffering with, he died from complications the disease brought with it. What killed him was a bleed on the brain due to the transfusions, which had weakened him and he had a massive epileptic fit and he crashed his head off something. I got a call from the hospital, and when I got there he was up and talking and he asked me to get him some fish and chips. Again, I thought he'd be OK. I went home, called the ward the next day at 6am and they told me he'd died during the night.

I was lost. I didn't say goodbye, and that hurt me. Then there was another problem: his funeral. I was the only one left at home, and so it came down to me to arrange everything. My head felt like it was going to burst. Then, after the funeral came and went I had a house and dog to look after. It wasn't my mum and dad's place anymore: it was mine. Some people would have thought of this as a benefit, and of course, if my head had been straight at the time it would have been, but it wasn't.

There was an occasion that I think even the dog realized there was something wrong, and he dog jumped onto my lap to comfort me. As much as I felt like crying, I couldn't. The weight of sadness was there, my heart was heavy, my head was in pieces, and I wanted so much to cry, but the tears just refused to fall. I felt like I had dried out. I got angry with myself and thought that I was so useless that I couldn't even do that right. How could I not be able to cry? I took myself off to bed, and that was when the darkest thoughts began to hit me.

It was a couple of months after dad went that I thought I couldn't be bothered with life anymore. I woke one day and realised I had to end the suffering, and so I had to think about how to do it. The first thing I had to do was find a way that didn't hurt, because I don't like pain. Jumping off a building was out of the question in case the fall didn't kill me. Cutting my wrists would also bring pain, so that too was out of the question.

By a simple process of elimination I came to the idea of swallowing a load of pills. That would mean I just went to sleep and never woke up. That became a constant thought that I couldn't get out of my head. I went into chemists and read the literature on the medication to see what was a dangerous level; I went online to search out what would be lethal and painless.

Then I began having blackouts. The odd thing here was that I wasn't a boozer or a toker, and never had been, so I couldn't blame it on the drink or wacky baccy. It was odd because I would be sitting on the sofa at 4 o'clock in the afternoon one day, and wake up at 3 in the morning not knowing what I had done or where I had been. That was worrying.

On one occasion I woke up at 2am in my front garden with no shirt on. I was lying on one side of the garden, the front door was open and the dog was lying next to me. I had no idea how I got there. The last thing I remembered before that was being with a mate 20 miles away in Chelmsford. I gave him a call the next day and asked what had happened the night before. He said I'd left him at half-past nine and everything was fine.

From having blackouts and thinking about suicide to actually doing it was only a short jump. Swallowing a stack of pills was the best way, however, getting enough of them wasn't so easy. If you walk into a chemist and ask for twenty packs of tablets the pharmacist is always going to ask you questions. I had to trawl around town on what I'd decided to call a "treasure hunt", and I went to every chemist I could find and bought as many codeine-based pills as I could get my hands on without being asked any questions.

I wanted codeine pills because they would put me to sleep before they killed me, and death would be painless. I ended up with 40 packets of pills. Incredibly, just knowing I had those at my disposal made me feel a lot better. I knew I had the means to off myself when the time came, and my mood brightened. It was comforting.

I used to line the boxes up and count how many I had of each type, but there were occasional visits from one of my sisters and I had to rush around and hide them in case she saw them. I was worried because one of my sisters is particularly nosey and I thought she might find my stash while she was doing the dusting or cleaning I might not have done. I decided I would write letters to my family members to let them know they had nothing to do with what I was about to do; that it was my decision, that I was an adult, and that they shouldn't blame themselves. I wanted them to know that they had done enough for me to know I was loved and cared for, and in the end I must have written a couple of hundred notes because I'd get something wrong in one of them and end up binning it and starting again.

This process too, was frustrating because yet again, I was cocking things up. How could I not get a suicide note right? What was wrong with me? How could I fail at that too? But I had to do it, because there was no way I could have any of them blaming themselves for something that was entirely my decision.

I got to the point where every day was going to be the day and then, for one reason or another it wasn't. I'd go to bed thinking, "Right, tomorrow", and then it wasn't.

Then I finally plucked up the courage decided I was going do it. Today was the day. The date was November the 8th, 2003. I'd had enough of messing around and I was fed up with the oohing and aahing of it, and so it would be today. I woke up feeling pretty good with myself and I was relaxed. There was a sense of happiness. I hadn't felt so happy for as long as I could remember. There would be no more messing about. I was ready. I got all the pills together and looked at them. Then I was worried that some of the pills might be of a chalky consistency and I wouldn't be able to swallow them.

It sounds comical when I think about it now, but I am the world's worst pill taker. If I have to take a chalky pill, it doesn't matter how much water I've got, the pill stays stuck at the back of my throat and I end up gagging, which would have been the opposite of what I wanted. I ended up grinding them up into a powder, and then I thought about the taste of them, and that the might be horrible and I wouldn't be able t handle it, so I got some cola and dropped a spoonful of the powder into it.

Of course, you've probably seen the Mentos mints clips on YouTube: well this was the same. The cola reacted and fizzed up, spurting all over the place, and while I can giggle about it now, it made me want to cry back then. Again, I had cocked it up and I was furious with myself. I ended up mixing the powder together with blackcurrant juice in a big bottle. I shook it and looked at it, but I couldn't yet drink it.

I felt a kind of peace come over me and I couldn't believe how relaxed I was. It was incredible. Strange. I sat there looking at the juice and then I began sipping it. It was such a lovely feeling. I had no thoughts about anything. Not my family, not my friends, not myself. Some people think it's selfish, but I didn't feel that way at all. For me at that moment, I felt like I had control of my life – what little there was of it left – and all my problems began melting away. Then I felt ill. The further

I got down the bottle the worse I felt. My head began throbbing and a massive headache came on and I felt sick. I carried on sipping the drink, but the taste got worse. Maybe there was some settlement of the powder. Then I vomited with such force it was like something out of a horror film. The anger I felt with myself was frightening. Again, I couldn't even get that right.

There was around a quarter of the bottle left and I forced myself to drink it, but as much as I swallowed, it wouldn't stay down. I puked and it spewed out of me. Then I felt so bad I called 999, and in what seemed like seconds later an ambulance was outside and I heard someone banging on the door. I felt dazed, not ill, and there were a couple of people there. They asked the usual questions, what I had taken and how many, and how much I'd drunk, had I vomited?

Christ, there were so many questions! I said that either they take me to hospital or eave me alone, so they took me to A&E, where a sister came and asked me, "Who's been a naughty boy?" Seriously? Then a doctor asked me why I had done it, but I couldn't answer anything other than it made me feel better. I had no emotions and I didn't want to be there. There was nothing to enjoy.

The toxicology test results came back and the doctor said I was fine, though he referred me to see the psychiatry team in the morning. That night in hospital was horrible. There was a huge amount of shouting going on, people pissing and shitting themselves, arguments going back and forth, then there was that awful National Health Service dinner-time smell that makes everyone want to puke, and as tired as I was, I couldn't sleep. It was like I was in stuck someone else's nightmare that I couldn't get out of. At one point I asked one of the nurses if they were going to give me a sleeping pill, and she looked at me like I was stupid. It was the first time I had smiled in I don't know how long. The irony!

As much as I was told I was lucky to survive, I didn't feel lucky, I felt angry. How crap must I be if I couldn't even kill myself? I was still in the same clothes I had arrived in. There was puke down my front, it was dirty, stained and it smelt hideous. When I spoke to the psychiatrist he asked me if I had asked for a sleeping pill and I had to explain I was kidding.

This guy looked like he was 12 years old, and while I respected him I didn't have a lot of faith in his ability to help me. The questions he asked I had no answers for. I had no relationship problems, no work worries, no family issues, I just felt shit. I had no answers. I was tired. When he asked if I would do it again I was honest and said I didn't know. I didn't. I had no idea. The only thing on my mind was to get back home and clean up in case my sister came and saw the state of the place.

When I got home the feeling of nothingness still hung over me, though I was thankful there was no explaining to do with my family, and I decided to go for a drive. I thought about selling the house. Maybe that was the start I needed? The change that could help me restart my life? While I drove I went to old haunts that I had gone to as a kid and it made me feel worse. In an hour I had gone from thinking about moving forward to depressing myself again.

As the days passed I seemed to get a little better, the blackouts stopped, the house went on the market, I went back to work and everything was good for a couple of months. Then I found myself walking along the promenade at 11 o'clock at night with no shoes or socks on. I had blacked out and the depression was back again. My head went to pieces. I had started to think I was OK, but there I was; stones between my toes, walking down a seafront 15 miles from where I lived, and I had no idea how the hell I had got there. I had my wallet in my pocket, but no car keys, so knew I hadn't driven there.

The last thing I recalled was being at work, so I had to do some detective work. I got a cab home and tried to work out what had happened. My car and my keys were there. I called one of my workmates and told him I couldn't go to work the next day, and also asked what time I had left work that day. He said I'd had a meeting in Southend, which explains how I got to the promenade, but I couldn't remember what happened afterwards, and why the hell was I shoeless?

I managed to get myself into a routine, though I still felt perpetually numb, and it was almost a year later that I tried to kill myself a second time. It was the 21st of October, and I'd been suffering for a few months. My house had been up for sale for some time, as the market was sluggish then, and while there had been interest, and at one point it looked as though the sale may go through. I was rethinking about whether I wanted to leave or not, and I was having odd feelings about selling. I had been seeing a psychiatrist, who had contacted my GP who put me on antidepressants. He said he felt that it was due to loss and bereavement that I felt as I did. I was on a low dosage, but over a period of time the dosage had been raised and during this year the blackouts had gone.

One night I went to a leaving do for a colleague. It was a barn dance and we had to dress as cowboys, and although I didn't fancy it, I went, but all the while I was there I wanted to get out. There were too many people around, and I felt out of place, not only socially, but of myself too. I left early, got home and I sat in the dark for a while. I felt cold in my head and I went to bed. When I woke the next day my head was in bits. The darkness was back again, and there I was, feeling nothing. I couldn't understand why, but I got it into my head that I was going to kill myself again. Having failed previously, I knew I had to bear whatever pain there may be, but I had to go through with it.

I drove to a place that I used to go to as a kid, Great Berry, which had lots of swings and slides in a park. It's on a big hill next to a road with a bridge. When I was a kid my dad used to tease me by telling me there was a monster under the bridge and we had to run to the other side or he'd get us. This time I thought to myself I would let the monster get me.

When I took my first step onto the bridge everything seemed like it was in slow motion. I could feel my heart beating. The odd thing was that it annoyed me and I wanted it to go away. I thought about which part of the bridge would be best to jump from and I made my way across and began striding back and forth from one side to the other. I began counting how long it took for a car to get from one point to another, so that if I timed it right, if the jump didn't kill me then the car hitting me would. It was like a double option: better than that, I would wait for a lorry. I felt at peace again.

I can even remember the smells of the place: at that time of year there was a bonfire smell and it took me back to my childhood. It was lovely. The bridge was pretty high and while the road had been busy as I walked toward it, once I got there, there was a sudden dearth of traffic, and there were no cars passing. There was only the odd one here and there, and definitely no lorries. I continued pacing, and trying to test how I could climb onto the top of the bridge cover without a driver seeing me if one approached. I wondered if I would sit, or would I stand, run, and then jump? All I could see was the bridge: it was like I was wearing blinkers, and I could hear only my heart beating. Out of nowhere I felt someone grab from behind and when I turned I saw the biggest policeman I had ever seen, and he asked me if I was OK.

He told me a concerned person who had seen me acting oddly had called him. I couldn't speak to him, and so he asked me to sit with him. I walked with him and sat at the side of the bridge for a while, and he asked if I had intended jumping. I said I had, and he asked me why, but I couldn't answer. We chatted, and while I understood why he was doing it, all the questioning got on my nerves a little. I know now that he did a great job helping me.

He told that if I was truly determined to kill myself in future then there was nothing he could do to stop me, but at that moment in time, there was, and so he asked me not to think about it for now. He also said that he'd been to a lot of families and had had to tell them that one of their loved ones had died. He'd done it with accidents, which was always horrible, but with suicides it was even worse, and the devastation it causes is horrendous. He said that it was down to people who felt like I did that he and his colleagues have to go to people's families and break news of a suicide, and he asked if I could really put him in apposition where he had to do that with my own family. It hurt me, but in my own head I thought they'd understand and get over it, like we do everything else.

I asked him what happens next, and he told me that I need more help. He took me to hospital and this time, thankfully, there was no, "Who's been a naughty boy," and I was admitted to a psychiatric ward. The psychiatrist accessed my notes and noticed I had been there before, and so he contacted my GP who told him I had attempted suicide previously.

This guy was really good with me; we chatted and he pointed out similarities in the attempts and how I could be helped. When I mentioned that it could be third time lucky, he said he wasn't going to allow that to happen. I spent four months in the psychiatric ward, and there was a lot of therapy and many talks, and there was no hiding from myself, which was a good thing.

I learnt to come to terms with the fact that I was depressed. The conversations we had were very painful, but also worthwhile. Exploring who you are and where you are is not always easy. My family didn't understand, mind you, neither did I! They had lots of questions that I couldn't answer, but I have to say that they were all there for me and they were a good network of support. Looking back, I can see that some of the signs were evident. I took days off work and gave stupid reasons and excuses, I withdrew from things I had done regularly and as normal, and I had much less contact with friends and colleagues. The purpose had gone from my life, and I felt less and less like I enjoyed it.

There was a moment of clarity, if you like. There I was, sitting on the floor, when I heard what sounded like creaking wheels and crockery moving, and saw a lady not wearing any uniform or lanyard, just in everyday clothes, pushing a trolley laden with drinks, cups and saucers. She noticed me in the corner and came over to hello.

She sat beside me, introduced herself and asked who I was. I responded, although truthfully just wanted to look away, but I felt like I ought to speak to her and be respectful. She asked me if I'd just arrived and whether I wanted a drink or something to eat, then went over to the kitchen area and got me a glass of fresh orange juice.

Then she sat beside me and asked me a few more things, like where I'd come from and just a little bit of general conversation. It wasn't in a prying way, but in a way of care. She listened to what I had to say and she didn't judge, it felt for a moment that I could really say what I wanted without any issue, so for me it helped me a lot. It was so nice that someone who didn't know me took an interest and treated me like a human, rather than a mental case. Although a small part of me wanted just to be left alone, I was also quite scared at being in a unit, and so she was a bit of a Godsend, really. I'm so grateful to her for doing that for me.

Some things have got better since that attempt to end my life. There is some help out there, however, due to being the way the NHS operates it's pretty much postcode led, and where some areas have loads of quick inroads for psychiatric care, others have long waiting lists and really very little in between. I have seen that GPs have got better at dealing with some of the issues regarding mental health and that's far better than that I got. I have also helped in my own area with some of the changes to mental health support and I think that is the key; that people who have been there and got the T-shirt, so to speak and work alongside health services to steer people towards the right kind of help that's on offer.

What I would really like to see is, firstly a mental health A&E, so that if someone is in crisis they would be able to go there straight there without the hassle of the physical health triage. You should be able to see someone qualified in mental health issues immediately, and that health and well-being lessons are taught at some point in school, and that coping strategies and speaking out about suicidal thoughts can be run of the mill and without social stigmas. If we put the subject out in the open there could be a lessening of fear of repercussions. Someone should be able to speak about how they feel, certainly if they feel like taking their own life.

If you want to help someone in the same position I was in, look at the smiles, and look at the eyes; if you ask how someone is, mean it when you ask. If you see major changes in someone's behaviour, chat with them. There's no need to offer advice, sometimes people don't want to hear that: they just want to know there is someone who knows they exist. When they say they're fine, ask if there's anything they might need, if there's anything you can do for them and tell them you're there for them: but make sure you mean it. Be the person they can call at any time, day or night, and always let them know that you will be there for them. I attempted to take my life but I have adjusted.

Nowadays I self-assess all the time. I think about why I didn't have that half-full thought strategy process. Although things might look bad, they can and do get better, or they can even just stay the same. At the time I was at my lowest, my own head couldn't get around the fact that things could get better, or even stay the same.

Some say suicide is a coward's way out, but I'm sure the people who say that have never been in a position where they want to end their life. It's not a coward's way out. Not at all. It's not the answer either, by the way! Far from it. I find that looking at times when I've been helped makes me want to help others, which is why I speak about my experience now. At some point in our lives we have had to reach out for help, and little acts of kindness go along way.

Mark Dale, 43, Essex

Six: Neil James, 49, Warwickshire,

I'm a 49 year-old ex-junkie and I am an alcoholic.

While I was at school I had a keen interest in photography. I loved the dark room work and my teacher told me if I kept up the progress of work I had been making there was no reason I couldn't be a decent photographer and could even make it my profession if I wanted to. Of course I did. A couple of years after I finished my O Levels I got a job at one of the top photography shops in Warwickshire. As it turned out, my snaps – more often than not landscapes – sold well, and I quickly became one of the lead snappers (I'm sure that term will annoy many photographers who prefer to be called 'togs') in the region. I did a ton of work ranging from weddings to portraits and wildlife magazines, and I won a couple of annual local awards from photography groups.

When Photoshop came out it revolutionised the way we photographers worked. I went digital the moment I realised it was going to be the future, and while the traditionalists stuck with film, I moved ahead as I could add even more scope to my work far quicker than I had ever been able to with the chemicals and dark room. My photos had a depth and striking aspect about them that made them sit head and shoulders above the rest. They had a really stark aura about them and very quickly I became sought after.

Adobe actually did me a favour because it priced plenty of people out of the competition as it was quite expensive software, and those of us who could afford it and use it to its full potential got the best jobs. When a guy from a design house came in to ask about his wedding photos I got speaking to him and he offered me a job on the spot, which meant I became a designer with very little training.

I grew into the position very quickly and the transition was smooth, and my eye for detail elevated me above the other designers. Another thing that helped me was that almost anyone with Photoshop and Quark (a new desktop publishing programme) knowledge and a Mac could almost name their own price with agencies or employers who needed us to do the work that the old printers used to do. It was the dawning of the digital magazine designer, the stuff I did ranged from vacuum cleaner bags to menstrual cycle item adverts (no name dropping here) and top brand cat and dog food for magazine adverts and tinned food labels.

The desktop publishing industry was on the cusp of a

boom, and it was around 1995 when Eddy Shah used laws that Margaret Thatcher had introduced a decade previously to break up the newspaper unions' stranglehold on the industry. The militant old union guys realised they couldn't throw a wobbler and make crazy demands of their employers anymore, or that they could call a strike for no reason other than they wanted a day off (an old hack confirmed this was the case with many one-day walk outs), and people like me were very quick to get in through the wide open and unpicketed doors of the newspaper industry.

I admired Shah for what he did, and I was lucky enough to find work on the *Today* newspaper, a national daily tabloid that he formed in the mid-eighties, even though when I worked there it was owned by Tiny Rowland's Lonhro conglomerate. The job was piss easy and the wages were great. I worked there for a year before it went bust in 1995, and then moved up to the North West.

After I made the move up north I hooked up with an agency and got good work and after six months I ventured out on my own. I'd met a dozen or so other designers whose work wasn't anywhere near the standard mine was but it was still decent enough, and they were getting plenty of contracts. My freelance work was also building so quickly that I could barely handle it, and I really was able to name my own price, sometimes I tried it on to see what I could get away with, and it was a rare occasion I lost the haggle.

There were a few other people I knew who had the same kind of skillsets that I had, and I decided to form an agency where the best of us could sweep up a lot of the work in the region and become the one company that everyone would use. Eleven other guys joined me and we called ourselves the Dirty Dozen, and we quickly gained a reputation as the best in the North West. Fast forward another six to eight months and I was pretty successful and earning really good money.

My bank balance grew very quickly and I began shopping at designer clothes shops. I bought Tricker and John Lobb shoes, Versace, Armani and Comme de Garcon shirts (OK, they were very over the top, but what the hell), I had suits tailored on King Street in Manchester, and I bought a new Rolex Submariner watch that a few years previously I could only dream of doing. The next step up the ladder was a three bedroom flat on a top floor warehouse conversion building in the up and coming part of Stockton Heath in Warrington.

I had been grafting in design for five years when I met Julie. I was at a book launch for a very famous Manchester band singer (who shall remain nameless) and after a couple of months of dating we hooked up permanently and she moved into my flat. We had been together for a further couple of years when she got pregnant, and while our social life had been a long party for quite some time, when Julie got pregnant she put a stop to her late nights but I didn't, and I spent far too much time partying while she was at home being the good expectant mum. We had a son who we called Christopher in September of 1997.

As much as I was overjoyed by his birth, I still went out partying far too much. I was too selfish and I wasn't anywhere near ready to settle down into a fatherhood role, and quite rightly, Julie became resentful and we began arguing. I used those arguments as an excuse to get out of the house and sink a few drinks. I'd also started snorting coke with the other designers in my team, and our partying went from nights out at the weekend to three day long drinking and snorting sessions, many-a-time we'd get no sleep and go straight from the nightclub to work and then back out again once we finished our workload. Julie was not best pleased!

It was credit to the skill and performance of the team that we were never sussed out by any of our clients, but our partying became a thing of legend among the designer fraternity. It got to the stage where people wanted to work with us for nothing more than the social side of things. I had mixed with a relatively famous band at one point, and my lifestyle was far more rock and roll than theirs had been. I earnt a lot more money than they did too! Our team worked hard and we partied very hard indeed.

There were plenty of times after a night on the tiles that I would walk five or six miles to get back home. I was so wired and I wanted to tire myself out so I could sleep for a couple of hours when I got home. It also meant that Julie would ignore me and I could go to bed without having to fight with her or justify what I'd done. There were many times I took detours to where the hookers operated and I'd go with one or two of them for thirty or forty quid for the pair. The worse they looked the more I liked them.

Eventually and (with the benefit of hindsight), completely understandably, Julie decided she'd had enough and she walked out on me, taking Chris with her. I could hardly blame her, even though in many of my drunken stupors I managed to convince myself I was the injured party. On the occasional dates Julie and I had gone out, they were never as a twosome; they were always with my team, and the nights would inevitably end up with me hurling abuse at her until she was in tears. It was no wonder that she left. After she went she gave me ultimatums about being sober whenever I had Chris, and for the first few times I managed it, but that soon went west.

Then a new guy, Ryan, started working with us and he and I got pretty friendly quite quickly. We had the same sense of humour, both supported the same football team and both liked the same music. The only thing we didn't have in common was that he was teetotal and he very quickly recognised that I had a drink problem, even though incredibly, none of the other team members could see it. It was after an office Christmas party when I was making a complete pest of myself that he had a go at me and told me I was a waster and no wonder my missus had walked out on me. It should have been a bit of a wake up call for me, though the next day I didn't remember any of it. The only reason I can relay it here is that I have heard the story told a number of times by those who witnessed it. Talk about embarrassing!

As it turned out, Ryan came to live with me while he was looking for a house to buy, and we got really close. While he lived with me I could control my drinking, and all we did was smoke a little weed while we watched films or TV. He was a bit of a guardian angel if I'm honest, and we had real heart-to-hearts and he could see I had demons living inside my head.

When he eventually bought his new house and moved out it hit me really hard. While he had been with me I had someone to answer to; to show that I was in control, even though it was really difficult to do so, he was the one thing that kept me from drinking myself into oblivion. He had been the closest thing to a brother I'd ever had, and once he moved out the last of his stuff, we had a hug, he told me he was always there for me, but I didn't know if I could handle being on my own again.

I'd arranged to have Chris one day, and I invited Ryan round to have dinner with us, and when he got to my pad I was pissed and he had a really hard go at me. He told me that if Julie ever saw that I was pissed it would be the end of seeing Chris again. He was right of course, and this was one of the things I admired about him, his ability to be completely honest with me, and still stay friends, even with all of my demons I carried around with me. I felt seriously shamed, which made me want to go and get drunk, and once he left, that's exactly what I did.

He came round to see me again a couple of days later and I was still drunk. I hadn't been sober since he left, and again he had a go at me, mentioning that if ever Julie came by on the off chance, I had to be compos mentis. She knew I was an alcoholic and if I fell off the wagon again while she was around, any modicum of trust she may have had in me would have been well and truly lost. Again, I knew he was right and again I was shamed into going out and drowning my sorrows and feeling sorry for myself.

My head began playing tricks on me too, and I got paranoid at so many things my work started to suffer. I had one contract that was worth around £250,000 a year and meant I could keep four guys in work, and when I turned up at the office I made a fool of myself and resigned, telling the company they could shove their contract up their arses. It wasn't long before one by one, the team drifted away and picked up the work my company was losing due to my drinking habits.

Ryan also went his separate ways as the company had gained such a poor reputation he needed solo work, and he had also hooked up with woman. He said that while he might not be around so much, he told me straight that he was there at any time of the night or day if I needed him. I had never felt so alone as when I used to go home to an empty house, even though I knew I didn't want anyone to be there to see me in the states I got myself into.

I got so smashed on so many occasions that I would wake up in hospital with a broken nose or teeth missing and my face in a mess, and I honestly didn't know if I'd been in a fight or had just fallen face-first onto the pavement. The amount of times I woke up and looked in the mirror to see a battered stranger looking back at me were uncountable. When I reflect on it now, I cannot understand how little I cared about how I looked. I would have seemed like a monster pitching to potential clients while my face was covered in cuts, scabs, dressings and stitches.

I met Ryan for a coffee one day and I'd bought a flask of Jack Daniels with me to pour into my drink. I made apologies and said I just needed it to straighten me out and stop the shakes, and he made me promise to go the next AA meeting, for which he had already got the times, and said he would come with me for moral support. That didn't go so well. I knew I had a problem, I knew I was an alcoholic and I knew if I didn't do something about it I wouldn't last much longer.

I had to introduce myself and tell everyone I was an alcoholic, and they took me through the steps, which were fine other than the God thing. I just don't get it. As hard as I've tried to connect I can't. I can't see what kind of God He must be if He allows the shit that happens in the world to happen. The excuse that man made it happen due to his inability to control his free will is just a lazy, crap cop-out. Still, I'd be a fool to dismiss it completely, and so while it may be true that I don't get it, it doesn't mean that I'm right.

Anyway, I didn't go to another meeting but I did get a slight handle on my drinking and went sober for around a month before I had a relapse that lasted for a week-long bender. Once again I was in a stupor. During the course of the previous year I'd not only gone through all of my savings, but I'd also maxed out my credit cards and remortgaged my pad to the tune of twenty thousand quid. I was in Shit Street.

There were a number of boozers I had run up tabs on, all of them had been asking me for a couple of weeks to settle up as it is illegal for a pub to give their punters a tab for the very reason that I was in so much hock with them. Legally they couldn't come after me, and although I wanted to settle, I didn't have the means to. I'd also got behind with my utility bills and I owed the gas, the electricity company, my phone supplier and the water board three or four month's worth of bills.

I applied for and amazingly, was granted another credit card with a ten grand limit, and for another short time I got off the booze again. That lasted for three weeks before I had yet another blazing argument with Julie over seeing Chris, and that was another excuse for me to get smashed out of my face again. Once I got mildly sober I felt the usual shame and loss of the small amount of dignity I felt I still had. I cried to myself for a couple of hours, wallowing in self-pity, ashamed and distraught. I couldn't see how I was going to straighten myself out. I'd gone from being the successful agency owner and earning stupid amounts of money, to a wreck who cold hardly get out of bed in the morning. I hadn't worked for six weeks or so and I had ignored all the calls had Ryan made, and whenever he knocked on my door I'd pretend not to be in until he went away.

Then I decided I didn't want to go on anymore. I'd been thinking about killing myself for a while, and the more I thought about it the better the idea seemed to be. What kind of dad was I? What kind of mate would ignore the one person trying to help him? What kind of man slaps his girlfriend around in front of his mates? What kind of bloke can allow himself to go from where I was two years ago to where I found myself at that moment?

The obvious thing was to put an end to everyone's misery, especially mine. For my first attempt I tried taking a bottle of pills I'd found at the back of the medicine cabinet that Julie had left from when she lived with me. I drank them down with a bottle of the cheapest vodka I could afford, though I woke up again in the morning with a filthy hangover, and though I didn't think it was possible, I felt even more self-loathing than I had the night before.

Then I decided I'd try starving myself to death, and do nothing but drink so that my liver would give out. As two weeks went past I lost a load of weight, though doing a great impression of a walking skeleton I realised it couldn't take the pain my stomach was giving me through not eating, and my diet became one of nothing but toast in the hope that my body wouldn't get enough nutrients to keep me alive. It didn't work.

On one of the rare occasions I felt like I might want to live, I made a plan of how I would get myself straight, which meant I had to stop drinking. I gave Ryan a call and told him I was OK but I just needed some space to get myself on track, and for a fortnight I got on track. I made a few phone calls, begged the remaining few former mates who would still answer my calls and managed to secure myself a couple of jaunts with some of my old clients and I thought I might be able to make it.

One thing in my favour was that I had managed to finish a contract and had even put some weight so I looked almost human again. Those jobs lasted three weeks in total though unfortunately for me, on the last day of the second contract I was invited out by one of the women I'd worked with before at the same client's office. She had no idea I was an alcoholic and I didn't want to embarrass myself by telling her. Apart from that I wanted to get my leg over too, as it had been so long since I'd had anything like a normal night of passion with someone who I didn't have to pay for it. Of course, I never got that far because, due to my liver not being able to process alcohol like a normal person's, I got pissed very quickly and ended up making a twat of myself and going home alone. I was off the wagon and back on the booze again.

The following days after I bought a couple of bottles of cheap vodka and drank myself stupid again. Once more I hated myself for the state I had got myself into, and I decided I would kill myself properly this time. I wrote a note to Chris to tell him I loved him and that my death had nothing to do with him, and I sealed in into an envelope and scrawled his name onto the front, then I wrote another to Ryan thanking him for being there for me, but that I just didn't have the strength or the will to get straight. I had another swig of vodka, finishing the last half of the second bottle in one go and looked around for a way to end it all. My flat had direct access to the roof and the bannister up to it had a rail on the stairs, and so I took a couple of wire coat hangers from my wardrobe, wrapped one of them around the top bannister rail and twisted it to the other, which I then put over my head and around my neck, squeezing it at the back as tightly as I could.

Closing my eyes, I jumped from the top stair and expected to feel a jolt and then dangle there and die in a short while, but because I was so drunk I hadn't tied the coat hangers together well enough, and all I did was to fall from the top to the bottom and hurt my back. I lay there for a while, crying to myself. Eventually I got up off the stairs and rubbed my neck, although I hadn't managed to kill myself I had done a really good job on injuring myself. It was really painful and I coughed so much I thought I might choke to death. After forcing myself to continue the coughing fit I realised that wasn't going to work either.

I crawled back to the top of the stairs, took the coat hanger from around my neck and twisted it once again with the other one, pulling on it to make sure it would work this time. Then I closed my eyes and jumped again. Again I got the same result. Again I found myself in a heap at the bottom of the stairs, crying because I was so fucking useless I couldn't kill myself because I was too wasted to be capable of even something as simple as that. I sobbed for ten minutes and then, out of both frustration and desperation I called Ryan, who drove over immediately to see me.

I sat there with my head in my hands, sobbing and feeling sorry for myself, and went through a list of everyone I could blame for me being in this shit position. I blamed Julie, I blamed one of my most reliable clients, I blamed other guys I worked with: I blamed almost everyone. Ryan sat there listening to my tirade of abuse. He didn't judge, he waited for me to finish and then we chatted, him talking straight and being completely honest with me.

He was probably the only person in the last seven years other than Julie who had been. He went through how I had behaved with her and asked me if I honestly thought I had been a good partner to her or dad to Chris. The strange thing was, and as much as I should have been able to see it, I was probably the last person I thought who should be on the list of blame for my situation. As I slowly sobered up, Ryan again took me through my shit list and we looked at the relationship I had with each of the people on it, and I finally saw it was me that I had the problem with, not with any of them.

Ryan said he would move back in with me to keep me on the straight and narrow, and we went to his house and picked up some of his clothes. He insisted on me going with him in case I tried killing myself again. That was the night I had my last drink. He got in touch with a couple of financial advisors and we met up with them a few days later. They gave me a couple of options and the best was to go for voluntary bankruptcy, which would alleviate the financial pressure on me, but would have repercussions that meant I would lose all my personal possessions that weren't vital, like my watch and the furniture in my house, and that got repossessed soon after too. I moved in with Ryan and began my recovery.

It's been twenty years since I had my last drink, and I have been working as a photographer for nineteen of those years. After my suicide attempt I spent a couple of weeks as a voluntary patient in a mental health unit and I got assigned a decent counsellor who was brilliant.

She helped me come to terms with who I was, that the past was gone and there was nothing I could do to change it, and that at some point in the future I could build a relationship with Chris. Sadly that hasn't yet happened and I have no idea where he is or what he's doing. I don't think it would be fair of me to get in touch with Julie and force her hand, but hopefully at some point when he gets an itch to look me out he either will or he won't, and I'm secure enough to accept it if he doesn't, though I hold out hope that he will.

One piece of advice I would offer to anyone considering taking their own life, is that no matter how desperate you think your position is, or how low you might feel, killing yourself is not the option you should take. I had no family to speak of that my death would have affected, and so the way I feel now has nothing to do with how others might feel or how I might have affected their lives. I have been as close to taking my own life as anyone could get, and I am glad I failed to do it. My life is on track, I will always be an alcoholic, but that doesn't matter, because every day I don't drink is another day I am proud of myself.

I count myself lucky to have had a mate that really did care when I was at my lowest point. I hope that if you're reading this that at some point, if needed, you can be that mate to someone who is in a similar position that I was, try to be there for them, no matter how hard they might make it for you to be so. The friendship Ryan and I have is indestructible, and I love him like he is my brother.

Neil James, 49, East Midlands

ABOUT THE AUTHOR

Andy Pacino is an education consultant currently operating out of Dubai, UAE. His expertise stretches from journalism to art consultancy, and authorship to education management.

His other books include:

Sir Alex, United and Me (Out of print)

SAS: First Man Through The Door (Out of print)

Sierra Leone: Deliver a Blow

I Was There When We Were Crap

Algunos Graciosos, Algunos No

Underground Gallery: Birth of a Movement,

Sometime Nonsense Means Something

50 Shades of Diversity

Shut Down The Crowd

The Horsetastic Adventures of Kass & Dandy

Coming soon:

The Rumblings of Thunder

Andy has also produced and directed documentaries on North West UK artists that include:

How Great Thine Art: Geoffrey Key

How Great Thine Art: Olivia Pilling

He also produced and directed the award-winning independent feature film:

Out of Court

www.ingramcontent.com/pod-product-compliance
Ingram Content Group UK Ltd.
Pitfield, Milton Keynes, MK11 3LW, UK
UKHW020417250726
13967UKWH00007B/2682

9 781739 909604